Tales of Love and Service:
Stories from the Heart

By John Gehring

COPYRIGHT

Copyright @ 2021 by John Gehring

Acknowledgement

The stories included in this book are part of a shared legacy created by individuals drawn together by a strong desire to serve and help those in need. I thank the thousands of volunteers, who as representatives of each religion and over 100 nations, embodied the role of ambassadors of peace and service on RYS projects and other good works. They are among the many noble people striving to live lives of meaning and consequence.

To put together these heartfelt stories, it took the inspiration and professional work of some wonderful people. Cheryl Roth gave the stories an audience through her work and personal mentoring that first found expression in her blog, nhfaithfusion.com. The tireless work of author, scholar, and friend Kerry Pobanz was critical in shaping the language and guiding each of the stories so that they could effectively convey the messages of love and hope that they offer. June M. Saunders, with her storytelling gift, imagination, and writing skill sculpted the characters of Juan and friends. It is amazing what she did with the lump of clay she was given.

Thanks to my wife Yoshiko and each of our five children, for they encouraged me and allowed me the freedom to write these stories and to spend countless days serving in the 60 nations where these stories were born.

To the founder and patron of the RYS, the late Dr. Sun Myung Moon, my deepest appreciation, as he provided an opportunity for so many to actualize the words of Dr. Huston Smith:

"Eternal gratitude towards the past.

Unlimited service in the present

Unbounded responsibility for the future."

TABLE OF CONTENTS

Author's Note

The stories or tales told in this book existed before they were given a voice by our storyteller, the Grandfather. Although the Grandfather is a fictional character, his experiences of love and service are real. They stem from true events during an international service program, the Religious Youth Service (RYS), which was founded in 1985 by Reverend Sun Myung Moon.

The unique program provided young adults from all nations, religions, and cultures the opportunity to live and share together while serving a community in need. This was in keeping with the founder's vision of the true spirit of religion transcending dogmatic strictures. Love, the end goal of all religions, is embodied and expressed through acts of selfless service. It is a love without boundaries or borders, a love that is the hope of the world.

The experiences and challenges of RYS team members living and working together as a small global community served as an instrument of healing and reconciliation of differences, both among the volunteers and the people they served. The experiences broke down language, cultural, ethnic, religious, and national barriers.

The RYS experience provided people with the opportunity to live up to their highest ideals in a group where this was a shared goal, even as the group's composition mirrored the world's diversity itself.

Those who gave of themselves during their weeks together discovered the wonderful truth that in giving, a person received. Such experiences helped transform the lives of many, motivating some to become lifelong champions of service to others.

Most of the stories shared in this book capture ways in which the power of love can transform hearts, lives, and communities in our increasingly interdependent world. The overall flow of the stories seems to follow an invisible compass, a compass that leads us to recognize how our shared destiny is tied to our ability to live as a global family.

American cultural anthropologist, Margaret Mead, offered an insight into the way history is shaped. Mead said:

"Never doubt that a small group of thoughtful, committed individuals can change the world. In fact, it's the only thing that ever has."

The role of the individual in inspiring and participating in a group like RYS or any other group devoted to service cannot be overstated. The power of a small group originates in a single person. Each of us carries within us the hope of initiating great and positive changes. A world of peace, love, beauty, and prosperity starts in the heart of each and every individual, and each person has the potential to make a great impact.

The stories of life and love that our storyteller offers are crafted in hopes of appealing to all those who seek and long for purpose, meaning, and value in their lives.

Since you are reading this book, we are confident you are that kind of precious person.

Introduction: These Times and Those

The Grandfather's stories largely involve people who were young a generation ago. The tempo of global transition was slower then, and some of the changes yearned for at that time have come to pass. Such shifts are reminders that change is indeed possible.

The speed and intensity of change have increased dramatically in recent decades. There is a growing recognition of interplay woven between systems that were once thought of as unrelated. We are growing sensitive to the enormous level of inter-connectedness on the micro and macro levels. A computer virus originating in Slovenia can quickly impact the industry in Japan, commuting patterns in Singapore, social relationships in Nairobi, and health care in Sri Lanka. As we have seen, a biological virus coming from a city in China can close a school in New York City, break a parent's heart in India, and set up a chain of economic losses that can sink major industries.

Opportunity and danger are running hand-in-hand, with the stakes of the race growing higher each day. How we adjust to the challenges should bring us to examine how our most cherished values can serve as part of a successful response.

Shifts in perception, attitudes, and understanding are part of the human condition. Our understanding of external things, both great (the universe) and small (the atom), alters with new scientific discoveries. Yet understanding the condition of the human heart is not quite so simple. What we do know is that human beings have a transforming ability to love.

Those who have pioneered the path of the heart, opening up to us the great potential that lies within its depths, may be the greatest of revolutionaries. We are indebted to them to the highest degree. In their wake comes a new and richer understanding of life and the whole of reality.

The people who figured in these stories are such pioneers of the path of the heart.

Philosopher Karl Jaspers recognized and named an "axial shift" during the six centuries preceding and including Jesus' lifetime. During that dynamic period, long-held tribal perceptions were challenged by great thinkers, reformers, and spiritual masters. As a result, cultures were reshaped for millennia by the words and personages of Buddha, Socrates, Confucius, Lao Tzu, Zoroaster, Moses, and Jesus. Walls and barriers that held people in relative darkness gave way to new light.

Teaching us a better way, these pioneers swam against the currents of their times. The words and lives of these master teachers pointed to true freedom. Among them, Jesus focused his teaching on revealing the sacred kingdom of the heart.

It is principally from the heart that great leadership emerges.

Jesus' words and example revealed a loving God as a Parent, patiently awaiting the return of His/Her children from a long and dangerous trip. The anticipation of this reunion is universally shared, no matter what terms one uses. The eyes of culture and religion offer varied interpretations of the same hope: humankind's return to a state of innocence, peace, and love.

The kingdom of heart that Jesus pointed to is one governed by love and service. Today's youth are among those most anxiously looking to create positive change. Some are working towards their dream by serving the poor and underrepresented; some are planting seeds through promoting education, and some are planting trees to revitalize the environment. Expressions vary, but the quest is similar.

Today, while confusion in the world of religion is problematic, we are also entering an era when good men and women of each religion, along with honest seekers and conscientious people of all kinds, are increasingly coming to recognize and appreciate the cultures of others. This process of discovery will lead to growing respect, trust, and cooperation between people of goodwill. In a sense, we are living in a unique time, one in which we can inherit the sum of the wisdom of the ages.

The penetrating words of Jesus — "I have come to serve, not to be served" — provide a timeless example of clarity in our quest to lead a good life. They challenge us by asking: How much am I serving and sacrificing for the sake of others? How much am I doing for the "least of these" — the poor, the downtrodden, the suffering, and less fortunate?

Jesus was not speaking to Christians. There were none in his day. He spoke to our shared condition as human beings.

Ultimately, labels matter very little, religious or otherwise. Our attitudes and actions toward one another matter immensely. In the end, it is our love for our fellow human beings, manifested in our actions, that counts.

Service is an indisputable reflection of the love that has the power to change the world. Welcome, then, to tales of love and service.

Part I: The Storyteller's Journey

Chapter 1: Juan Meets the Grandfather

"In a gentle way, you can shake the world."
Mohandas K. Gandhi

"Juan!"

Juan sat up in class and tried to look attentive. He had been dreaming, that was for sure. What had the teacher been saying? He heard other students start to snicker.

The teacher smiled benevolently.

"How old are you, Juan?"

"Sixteen."

"That's an age for dreaming," the teacher commented. "What were you dreaming about?"

Mr. Bennet's eyes were sparkling as if he knew the answer was the name of a girl.

Juan searched for words. Since he was probably going to get in trouble anyway, he decided to be honest.

"I was thinking of how I would like to make a difference in the world—make things better. You know, with all the war, and economic problems, and governments not being effective." He trailed off. "You know," he said lamely. He didn't dare to finish his thought: "I want to do something great."

The class was silent. Mr. Bennet looked surprised.

"Well, I guess you were listening, Juan, because that is exactly what I want this class to do. In our own small way, we are going to make the world a better place through service projects here in our community."

Juan's mouth dropped open as he realized he was off the hook. Mr. Bennet moved among the class, soliciting suggestions for service projects. There were usual ideas—a neighborhood trash clean-up, raising money for a charity through a bake sale, volunteering at a nursing home. Juan stifled a yawn. Not that those things weren't worthwhile, but he could tell the enthusiasm in the room was low.

"Those are all good suggestions," Mr. Bennet said. "Yet I think I detect a slight lack of inspiration here. I'm sure you will all do the work because if you don't, you will be marked down on your Civics grade. But if you only do it reluctantly, out of duty, I'm not sure you will understand the true meaning of service. Believe me, when you serve, you receive more than you give. And service is the way to change the world, even starting small, in your own community."

The teacher thought for a moment and cast his eyes over the students, who were trying to look alert and interested.

"I'll tell you what," Mr. Bennet said. "I want all of you to visit a man I call the Grandfather. He has been involved in service all his life, and he has plenty of tales to tell. Juan, can you visit the Grandfather at the address I give you and ask him if he will speak to a class of students on the value of service? He can do it in his home. He's getting up in years now, and I don't think we should ask him to come to the classroom. It's extra credit for you, Juan, if you arrange that."

Why does he keep picking on me? Juan wondered as the bell rang and the students gathered their things and started shuffling out of the room. He waited at the teacher's desk for the address. He needed the extra credit; that was for sure. When his father had died recently, Juan had missed some school—and when he had been at school, he had been hard to put to pay attention. The teacher handed him a scrap of paper.

Mr. Bennet said, "Juan, you may wonder why I keep singling you out."

Should he admit it? Juan started to shake his head to deny it, but instead, he met the teacher's eyes in affirmation.

"Sometimes," Mr. Bennet said, "we have longings that we can barely put into words — and we wouldn't even try, for fear of others laughing at us. We yearn to do something wonderful in the world, but we're afraid we might fail or look bad in people's eyes. Sometimes, though, a major life event can change everything in us so that we are ready to overcome our fears and go forward into making our dreams come true. Sometimes, when we lose someone important to us, like a parent, it can make us wonder with greater urgency what life is all about and what we are meant to do in this world."

At Mr. Bennet's tone of understanding, Juan ducked his head to hide the tears that suddenly sprang into his eyes. He missed his father so badly, sometimes his heart physically ached.

"Go see my friend, the Grandfather," Mr. Bennet told him, putting a hand on his shoulder. Juan mumbled a thank you and stumbled out, trying to make out the address through his misting eyes.

Mr. Bennet added, just as Juan was going through the door, "The Grandfather knew your dad."

That was a big impetus for Juan. He made the journey to "the Grandfather's" home right after school. The neighborhood indicated by the address was within walking distance. Juan neared an area of town where simple homes with well-kept gardens were located near newly constructed condominiums and apartment houses. He tried to picture how it might have looked in the years when his father knew the Grandfather. He knew his father had participated in some overseas projects years ago. That must have been when the Grandfather knew him.

The older homes fit more closely to Juan's imagination of the neighborhood back then, and he sensed he was nearing his destination.

Juan approached an elderly couple who were walking in his direction. He gave them a polite smile to disarm fears and create goodwill. Words were harder to find. How could he say, "I'm looking for the one they call 'the Grandfather'?"

Instead, he blurted out words about a service project, the Grandfather's participation in many of those, and the old man's potential ability to inspire Juan's class. The wave of words surprised the couple, but they seemed to understand.

The lady returned Juan's smile.

"Young man, from what you just told me, I think you are in the right place. That person working on his garden over there sounds like the person you are describing. It has been rather quiet at that house for some stretch of time, so I expect he will be happy to see you."

With a quick nod of appreciation, Juan shifted his undivided attention to the old man on his knees, working in the garden.

Hearing Juan approach, the old man looked up and offered a toothy smile that nonetheless lit up his whole face. Juan relaxed a little. The Grandfather's blue eyes offered warmth; at the same time, there was a penetration in them that seemed to Juan to bore into his very self. The keen eyes seemed to see things Juan was hoping to keep hidden: intentions, attitudes, concerns, hopes, and doubts. The Grandfather's eyes made Juan want to check his motive for coming there as surely as if a policeman challenged him to explain why he did not fully stop at a stop sign.

Yet there was something else about those eyes, Juan noticed. They had the luster of a dreamer. The Grandfather's eyes looked as if they had searched for the unseen treasures of a world filled with things like love, spirit, soul, and the source. Because of this luster and a searching quality, the eyes in the old face were young. It was as if, in remaining faithful to the dreams and ideals of youth, the Grandfather could continue to see things anew.

The old man rose from his knees, dusted his hands off on his pants, and said, "Come in, I have something for you," as if he had been expecting Juan.

The magnetism of the old man's presence overcame any hesitancy on Juan's part. He followed the elderly man into his house, stepping into a carpeted room filled with wooden carvings, cloth tapestries, awards, certificates, dolls from all around the world, and an accumulation of gifts ranging from Indian elephants to serene Buddhas.

"Please sit and share some tea with me," the elderly man invited.

Juan began to introduce himself, and yet another smile embraced him. "I know who you are. You look very much like your father, Juan."

Juan also smiled at the recognition, but his voice saddened as he told the elder man of his father's passing. The Grandfather nodded sympathetically.

"Juan, I am sure you know it already; your father was a very special man. I look forward to a time when I will share with you some of the stories he played a role in creating. Your dad and I spent nearly ten years together on service projects around the world."

"I think I remember him talking about you," Juan nodded.

After a few minutes of preparation, the old man served Juan tea, which they sipped together in the colorful room. Juan glanced around.

"Were all these things gifts from the people you served?" he asked.

"Yes," nodded the Grandfather.

"They're really nice," said Juan.

"Yes," said the Grandfather. "They are precious. But more precious are the internal gifts the people gave me." He looked at Juan keenly. Juan's eyes sparked with interest, and the Grandfather explained.

"As I've grown older, I've tended to bury the stories of my journeys within my heart. Perhaps it is a sign of growing wisdom that I have developed a greater discernment as to who to share my stories with. I only tell those who show signs that the stories can be appreciated for their inherent value."

Again, his eyes asked Juan a question.

Juan answered softly, "Tell me about the internal gifts they gave you."

The Grandfather smiled and nodded.

"Faith, for example, is a precious gift given to some. Yet love, the most precious gift, can belong to us all. Our relationships with others, both great and small, is the arena where love is earned and plays out. In that arena, those who live by love share in the fruits of love, enjoying peace, happiness, and the fullness of life together.

"Those were the gifts I received from those I served. I have had the honor of being inside the hearts and homes of many beautiful people all over the world, many of whom treated me as a brother. On numerous occasions, I received and shared food and hospitality and joined in on traditional music, games, and spiritual ceremonies that were a special part of daily life. One moonlit night, next to beautiful Lake Atitlan in Guatemala, which is nestled inside a volcano, I and others joined the local Mayan spiritual guide (shaman) in a sacred harvest ceremony, an unforgettable taste of the timeless. I felt I had touched a sense of eternal unity with those people — relative strangers to me, most of them."

Juan felt thoughtful. He gazed at a marked map on the wall. He rose to look at it.

"Honduras, Suriname, and Paraguay. Were you in those places too?"

The Grandfather nodded.

"And what did you do there?" Juan asked, taking up a cookie the Grandfather had provided along with the tea.

"Often during the day, I could be found laboring with my team and community members. We would be building or improving schools, community centers, and medical facilities throughout the day and would then share stories by a campfire under a star-filled, night sky."

"You've had a lot of adventures," Juan said in admiration. Looking at the world map made him feel restless as if he wanted to explore new lands. Looking at the old man's hand as he pointed to places on the map, Juan saw they were work-scarred.

"I was a friend of some in Australia's aboriginal community," mused the elderly gentleman, "and I literally rubbed noses with the Māori people of New Zealand."

The Grandfather wrinkled up his nose and shook his head gently as if he were rubbing noses with an invisible native.

Juan laughed. "Wow," he said. "You've been around. Where else have you worked and visited?"

"I loved Sri Lanka for its natural beauty, especially the beauty of its people, the Sinhalese and Tamil, who warmed my heart. The victims of the very violent civil war there opened their homes and hearts and, in the process, learned to forgive and move forward. Seeing Tamil and Sinhalese work hand-in-hand in the service of a poor community and finish that work with a warm embrace seemed to me to be the ultimate cure for war. I felt I was part of a healing legacy."

"Wow," said Juan. "That must have been intense."

"Yes," the Grandfather said softly. "It was. Then, of course, Africa called to my soul often, with a mother's voice. In South Africa, I enjoyed training and working with the youth of Soweto Township as well as with those living in overcrowded urban homes and neighborhoods in Cape Town. Part of my work at the Cape focused on maintaining the unique natural environment of that ecologically sensitive region while we painted and made local community improvements.

"In Ghana, Nigeria, and Uganda, I labored with friends on efforts to build schools and an agricultural center. My role was often a small one, but, like every small part, it had meaning and value. My life's journey provided me the opportunity to offer a willing hand to returnees (those who put down their guns to return home) from the wars of Northern Uganda. That was where I got malaria. Malaria is so much a part of life in Africa I am actually proud to be able to share that condition of suffering with my African friends."

Juan felt a sense of wonder. This man had not only experienced the world; he had encountered its dangers too.

"The voices of India called me often and pulled me back to her people, again and again," the elderly man mused reminiscently. "The voices represented India's stark contrasts. One voice was filled with an earthly, rude hardness. It scratched the eardrum with urgency and seemed to pierce illusions and ground the listener to cold realities. Another voice, soft, alluring, mystical with a tangible beauty, offered hope. This subtle sound found ways to move through my whole being and rest my heart."

The Grandfather grew silent, seeming to look down the years spread before him in his imagination. He roused himself from the reverie.

"India drained me. It took all my effort and challenged my senses, yet the paradox that is India, in fact, left me with more than I came with. Imagine the opportunity to mingle with 'Untouchable' families, those forbidden entries into 'regular' society by the weight of the region's lingering caste system. I readily entered these families' small, hut-like homes that stood alongside unpaved roads just a few hundred meters away from the much larger homes, paved roads, and shops where the 'regular' families lived."

"'Untouchables'?" Juan asked.

"Yes, they are the lowest rung on the social ladder. Outcasts. Everyone thinks they are in their lowly position because of something they did wrong in a previous life, so they are considered unclean. There are millions of such outcasts in South Asia. For me, it offered a bitter but important life lesson. Every society has its outcasts. In a way, India has been simply more honest about theirs. Developed societies look down on people of different skin colors, ethnic backgrounds, religions, the poor, and people in low-status jobs. Yet they are all human, all infinitely precious. We degrade ourselves when we degrade them."

"What work did you do in India?"

"During volatile times of rioting in the streets of Delhi, when tension between Muslims and Hindus were explosive, we guided workshops on reconciliation. People's positive responses to this served as a light of hope through the turbulent days ahead. This led to further efforts at encouraging religious cooperation through having multi-religious teams work on repairing Hindu holy sites, a Christian church, and a local mosque, and doing community work at a Gurdwara. At one point, with international volunteers and social service students from Gandhi University, we had 100 young adults from 12 nations. It all gave me so much hope.

"Yes, sometimes I feel I have been everywhere in the world. While swimming and snorkeling with the multi-colored tropical fish amidst the captivating beauty of the Micronesian island of Palau, I felt an overwhelming awe. I felt I had been given a passage into a part of the Kingdom of Heaven. In an emotional contrast, on my journey through the islands of the South Pacific, I caught a sense of the unfathomable loneliness that can be a companion for those living on a small, isolated island surrounded by an expanse of sea. I've been to Samoa, Tonga, Hawaii, and other islands where the beautiful people there taught me both to work and play.

I worked in Belfast, in the north of Ireland, or Northern Ireland, depending on your politics. On a rainy day, I could be seen working on a peace garden with English and international volunteers alongside local Catholic and Protestant residents. Despite it being in the 'Times of the Trouble', they could be heard joking and sharing with each other.

"Laughter! It is the universal language, Juan, and you would be surprised how many laughs you can share with people, even when you don't speak the same language.

"I was also in Eastern Europe after the collapse of the Berlin Wall in 1989. As nation-states burst out of an era of state rule, they began to enter an age of freedom. I was grateful to play a role in guiding hundreds of volunteers to that region, where they could work together to discover and create meaningful ways to contribute to the quality of life in the newly liberated countries.

"I witnessed the too-common scenes of forlorn children—dirty, belly-swollen, wide-eyed children from all corners of the world, calling out with both physical hunger and a hunger for love. Etched in my heart are conversations with those who suffered from war: the widows, the orphans, the refugees, and the homeless—those too familiar with the depths of sorrow.

"Yet I also recall the jubilant dancing of Ethiopian refugees in Italy, the harmonious singing of groups of Tongan villagers, the sounds, sights, and motions of the drummers in Bogo, Uganda, and a time when villagers lined the roads to sing, dance, and give welcome. When

Mideast violence filled the headlines, I would recall the warm embrace of Arab and Bedouin families sharing a welcome meal, proving to me over and over again why Arab hospitality is globally recognized. I met young artists advocating for peace at their kibbutz in northern Israel in the plain sight of neighboring Lebanon.

"In spite of what I have seen of poverty, suffering, war, and deprivation, I believe that the many good people, closely linked by recognition of the same living God, are going to realize that our ultimate happiness is tied directly to the well-being of our neighbor. One simple moral imperative serves as my North Star, a guiding light where I can put my trust: Give to others, especially to those in need. Do this to show people the true nature of God, our loving Parent."

The sun was beginning to set as the two men, young and old, sat in the gathering shadows.

"I imagine you will need to be getting home," the Grandfather said to Juan. "I'd like to get to know you better, although I must say: you resemble your father so closely, I feel like I already know you. Of course," he said stoutly, "you are your own person and your own man. Now, before you leave, I want you to pick out a gift for yourself from among my things here."

"No, no, I couldn't," said Juan, waving his hands in protest.

"I will be offended if you do not let me give you a gift after you have given me the gift of your time."

"No, I really couldn't—" protested Juan.

The Grandfather looked at him keenly and then went over to his bookshelf. There was a golden globe on it, intricately engraved and set in a polished wooden base. Juan had to admit he had been eyeing it.

"I saw you admiring this," said the Grandfather. "So, this is the gift I will give you." He burst into merry laughter. "I give you the world!"

"Thank you," said Juan fervently, joining in the Grandfather's infectious laughter. Then he hesitated. "Would you like to give the world—as you have seen and experienced it—to my class? I'm in Mr. Bennet's Civics class, and he said that we could spend this semester listening to you, if you would agree to it, about your service all over the world. We are going to create a local service project, and he thought—"

"Yes, of course," said the Grandfather. "Tell Mr. Bennet to call me to arrange things. He has my number. He could have asked me himself—but he chose to give me the gift of you. You know, Juan, you are a gift to the world. Everyone is. Give of yourself, and you will understand the depths of your infinite value. As Gandhi said, 'In a gentle way, you can shake the world.'"

Juan didn't understand why, but he felt his heart swell inside him. The indefinable something he had been searching for, longing for in his heart, had been filled by this visit with the elderly gentleman. It was all mingled up with how much he missed his father and how much he wanted to be like him. He felt an urge to hug the old man, but he wasn't sure that would be proper. He ducked his head in a way that he hoped showed respect, and the Grandfather embraced him after all.

As the Grandfather wished him, "Goodbye, son," Juan almost thought he heard the voice of his father in the old man's voice. He put on his sunglasses as he left home, even though it was dusk, so he could walk home without anyone seeing his tears.

Chapter 2: The Grandfather's Dream

"Hold fast to dreams, for if dreams die, life is a broken-winged bird that cannot fly."

Langston Hughes

At the prospect of speaking to a whole class of young people, the Grandfather felt both hope and fear. He hoped the tales he told them would give life, joy, inspiration, and comfort. He hoped that the stories would take on a life of their own, being repeated to others by his listeners. His biggest fear was being ignored, tuned out by a bored younger generation, his stories and the nobility of spirit they represented dying within him as their attention focused on things more mundane and of questionable value.

For several nights before the students came, the Grandfather had a recurring dream. In it, he had stepped outside of himself and had become an observer of the passing of time. Seasons approached in rapid succession; in a breath, they came, went, and returned, like the seasons of his life.

The dream was giving him anxiety, as it was accompanied by a heavy feeling of sorrow. He saw in it successions of travelers passing his home, neglecting to stop, unaware anyone was even there. It was as if the entire world were passing him by, no longer considering him or his experiences to be of value.

The Grandfather was not one to wallow in the helplessness and anguish he felt as a result of the dreams. He had seen too much of goodness and divine intervention to give in to that. Yet the dream carried with it a sense of wasted opportunity, something precious lost, something offered without a chance to be received. As he watched a continuous flow of people passing his home in his night-time visions, some journeying alone, others traveling in groups, he could hear their conversations. He observed that many of those who passed by seemed to see life simply as an adventure. On this adventure, some walked eagerly with a sense of secure invincibility, whereas others, in contrast, limped as a result of past injuries that had never found proper healing.

Where were they all going? From his perspective, to navigate the journey of life, it was essential to have an internal moral compass to guide one. Yet, many had not paid attention to that essential detail. They were all going somewhere in a hurry, but where were they going and why? Did they themselves know?

He knew there was a treasury of timeless wisdom, both sacred and secular, and the advice of sage people with experience and generosity available for all the passersby. Yet they traveled on, not recognizing the potential gifts. They seemed to own an arrogance bred out of ignorance that there could be so much more to life than simply hurrying by each day.

He watched in the dream as the travelers kept adding unnecessary things to their loads, while any person who had been deep into the journey could have told them these things would only become burdens before the trip's end. They simply did not realize what good, beautiful, and true things could fill the vacuum of material possessions if they spent less time pursuing them.

The Grandfather tried to conjure up ways to gain the attention of those who were passing. He could not. They seemed complacent and unconcerned that their journeys were going nowhere. As he dreamed, his internal anguish grew. No one was listening, no one cared. Apathy, which the Grandfather considered the greatest enemy of love—not hatred, but apathy—showed on their faces.

He found himself praying, "Please don't let the stories stay locked forever inside me, the characters' life tales unable to walk in the consciences of others. Please, young friends, come and give new life to these stories and see, please, how they can give life to you."

Then, soon, the dream became real. There were travelers on the road, but these travelers came inside the gate and knocked on his door. Foremost among them was Juan, whose face was full of hope and anxiety.

Mr. Bennet waved from behind the knot of beautiful young people, calling out to the Grandfather in greeting.

Momentarily, the Grandfather thought of a line of poetry from Langston Hughes: "Hold fast to dreams, for if dreams die, life is a broken-winged bird that cannot fly."

Inspired, the Grandfather cried out heartily in welcome: "Well, what do you say, young men and women? Do you have time in your busy schedules to taste a tale or two? I have stories that may be of help to you on the journeys that lie ahead of you. Shall I introduce you to worlds unknown, from a different age, yet real and flush with the blood of life and the taste of adventure? Shall we turn the pages of recent history while enjoying the taste of a cup of Himalayan tea or Guatemalan coffee? Come in, come in!"

The students laughed and nodded appreciatively, murmuring polite thank yous as the Grandfather stood aside to let them enter. It was gratifying to hear the exclamations of those who were already inside as they looked at his collection of gifts and mementos from all over the world.

Juan jumped in to help serve coffee and tea as well as pass out tins of exotic biscuits. The Grandfather looked at the bevy of young faces above the teacups and dessert plates. They looked at him so expectantly, in polite silence. He did not want to fail them.

He stood tall before them.

"First," he said, "First, I think I must introduce you to a lady you have heard of but do not know. She is a lady who has been all over the world, in every hut and hovel and in the eyes of hungry infants. It is she who dogs the steps of children as they walk miles to get a simple bucket of water; as they die of diseases, you were inoculated against as toddlers or have never even heard of before. She is the lady who follows them as they go without shoes, without care, and all too often without food. Indeed, this lady is the mother of many, many suffering children throughout the world."

"What is her name?" asked one of the male students.

"Her name is Lady Poverty."

Part II: Lady Poverty

Chapter 3: Buckets of Teeth

"As we lose ourselves in the service of others, we discover
our own lives and our own happiness."
Dieter F. Uchtdorf

The students were silent, gazing expectantly at the Grandfather.

"We will not glorify the lady, as she is the cause of so much suffering and death," the Grandfather said. "Indeed, Lady Poverty is no one's friend. In some areas of the world, her deadly reach is immeasurable.

"I will show you the fatal grip of Lady Poverty when we take you to a region in Uganda. There 25% of the children are dead before their sixth birthday, in large part because of untreated malaria. You will see the harsh lady's power as a poor father wrestles with his conscience when faced with a decision to pick up guns or silently watch as his children face starvation. We will meet Lady Poverty as she hovers over a mother in the Philippines who watch her baby die of hunger—but only after she fed the baby the only thing she had to eat—newspapers. We will uncover some of Lady Poverty's dark enigmas as we learn of children who are kidnapped, not for ransom, but for the sale of their body parts."

Some students gasped.

"Yes, Lady Poverty creates tragic situations in which indifference plays a part. Yet, her grip cannot permanently crush the human spirit.

"When humanity links the quest for truth and justice to a willingness to serve, hope grows. When we as people make sharing and cooperation the norm, we seize the future from her grasping hands. I hope we can work together to protect the future from her viciousness. What is more, as an aviator and spiritual leader, Dieter F. Uchtdorf said, 'As we lose ourselves in the service of others, we discover our own lives and our own happiness.' Service not only helps those we serve; it helps us too."

He cleared his throat and began.

"One day, a group of young people, not unlike yourselves, were in Das Marinas, Philippines, a community filled with unemployed and underemployed men and women. In the neighborhood, there were many children and elderly who suffered from malnourishment. Daily life was filled with difficulties, but many children found an escape through eating sweets filled with processed sugar. Processed sugar is very harmful to the teeth, and in the community, many people had mouths full of cavities.

"Few families had the funds to visit a dentist, and almost no one had money to pay for full and proper treatment. Without proper treatment, cavities get larger and larger. In time, the decay can expose nerves and send out waves of pain that can be close to maddening.

"In sharing with local children and their families, we heard and witnessed the suffering that people were dealing with on account of dental problems. Several parents asked us if there was something we could do to help. We responded by sending a request to Japan in hopes of soliciting a dental team from our sister organization, the International Relief Friendship Foundation (IRFF). The IRFF team in Japan regularly sent out medical teams to poorer nations in Asia. To our relief, they shared that they were planning on sending a dental team to the Philippines, and the team would squeeze Das Marinas into their tight schedule.

"Japan has state-of-the-art medical facilities, and this is what our team of professional dentists was used to.

Their regular customers had the luxury of being able to return week after week until their treatment was completed. This was not the situation they would be facing in Das Marinas. Our barong (village) could offer no such places for them to do their craft. All we could manage was to set up an impromptu outdoor office under a canvas canopy over a basketball court to shield the patients and doctors from the blazing sun or pouring rain.

"The dental team was under time constraints and could spare only a single day in Das Marinas. Of course, the dental options of a single day of treatment are extremely limited. Yet, for those who were suffering from toothaches, a single treatment could offer them relief from intense pain.

"Understanding their limitations, the medical team discussed options and shaped a plan of action. The team would utilize that day by focusing treatment on those suffering from severe pain. In most of the cases, the only course of action they had was to simply remove teeth in a proper medical way.

"On Dental Day, we announced, we would provide free dental service as a gift from our friends from IRFF-

Japan. To get the word out, we shared the news with some of our neighbors and asked them to spread the news by word of mouth. You would be surprised how well communication happened in an era before cell phones!

"The news spread. One family got excited and told a person who worked in the local radio station. Before long, Dental Day was being announced on the radio as a public service announcement. Community anticipation of Dental Day grew. For many, this was going to be their first visit to a dentist.

"The open-air environment of our improvised clinic allowed breezes to keep the work area a little cooler. Unfortunately, the open-air also allowed various flies and bugs to join us.

"When Dental Day arrived, long lines of people of all ages began to form hours before the early morning opening. It was becoming clear that the dental team would be pushed to their limits to meet the community's expectations.

"When the first patient sat and opened her mouth, the dental team went to work. People continued nervously sauntering into the outdoor clinic as the lines took on special identities. A line was dedicated to those waiting to be checked, a second line was for those about to be worked on, and a third line would later form to handle the after-care patients. Sitting in a central location were three improvised dental chairs dedicated to those who would be having teeth extracted. Next to the extraction chairs were metal buckets that would serve to hold removed teeth.

"With care and persistence, the dental team checked patient after patient: squirmy young children, elderly men, and anxious mothers. A weather-beaten grandma displayed a row of decayed teeth lining her lower right jaw.

"Time passed, and the heat grew in intensity. Patients sat down on the improvised chairs and received a prognosis that was almost always in favor of extraction. Almost every patient added their extraction to the pile of teeth in the buckets.

"As the day wore on, the buckets continued to fill. The uneven piles of teeth and bloody spittle presented a disturbing visual image. Yet, through the blood and spittle, some noble service was being done. Some pain was being taken away.

"The day stood in stark contrast to the daily office routine in urban Japan. While in Japan, our dental workers were in sanitary, white state-of-the-art dental offices, whereas now they sat in simple wooden chairs a few meters away from buckets filled with teeth, blood, and the spittle of surgery. As the day progressed, flies swirled in increasing numbers. The dentists seemed unstoppable, only pausing to swat at flies, drink water, or take a brisk walk to use a neighbor's outdoor toilet.

"Despite the mess, it was a day of relief. The people of the community were relieved from the continued pain of aching teeth and the ailments linked to drastic tooth decay. In a sense, the buckets of teeth were a cause to celebrate. The dental team served as liberators; their bloody work was releasing the patients from daily agony.

"We measure a day's success from various points of view. For soldiers on the battlefront, it may be the fact that they, along with their mates, made it safely through a tough day. For the businessman, success could be the closing of a big deal. For the artist, success might be the visual creation of an image or experience long held in the imagination.

"Our dental team found solace and satisfaction in three buckets of decayed, extracted teeth. They realized the situation they faced was regrettable, but they dealt with it as best they could. As the dental team sipped their tea in reflection at sunset, you could read on their faces a warm satisfaction for doing something out of the ordinary."

The Grandfather looked at the circle of young, somber faces. He knew his story had hit home. He could almost see the ambitions forming in the youthful hearts: "Maybe I should become a dentist or doctor and do something noble like that."

"Next week, when you come again, you will become better acquainted with Lady Poverty and her lack of mercy in our world. Until then, young friends, I bid you farewell."

The spell broke, the students murmured among themselves and rose to bring their cups and dessert plates into the Grandfather's kitchen. Several made quick work of the dishes as their fellow students thanked the Grandfather and said their goodbyes.

Juan spoke up, "Mr. Bennet, may I catch up with you in a few minutes?"

Mr. Bennet glanced from Juan to the Grandfather, who nodded.

"Yes," Mr. Bennet said. "Don't linger long, though. I have to have everyone present and accounted for back at school."

When everyone had left, Juan shyly asked the Grandfather to tell him something about his father.

"That is, if you're not too tired," Juan said solicitously.

"Tired? No, I'm energized! I've wanted to tell my stories, and your classmates were very attentive.

"Your father, Juan, could follow directions, but if you gave him the freedom to figure things out and offer his own creative solutions to a problem, he most often did an excellent job. Part of his success in leading was his ability to talk to different people and really try to listen to both the things they said and the things they didn't say. He understood human nature well and grasped the wisdom that silence often speaks louder than words. I think you have that quality too.

"I imagine, like him, you do not like to waste time, probably because you sense that you have important things to do in your life. While your dad valued his time, he freely offered his help to others. I think he realized that was one of the best uses of his time, taking care of others.

"Your dad liked to have fun and could get others to invest their time and energy into things. He clearly wanted to do good, and had an ability to find ways to make it fun. A jokester at times, he avoided the type of humor that tears at people, for he had a gift in that he could laugh at himself and others with equal passion."

Juan nodded. "Yes, he was like that."

"I think you have many of the same qualities, Juan. In fact, I was wondering if you might have some ideas as to how to make these class meetings a little more fun for the students, or at least—to bring in other elements. Of course, I want to share my stories, but I want to share them in an atmosphere where people's hearts are open, vulnerable in a way."

"I was thinking—" Juan paused shyly. "I mean, I was considering asking you—of course, I'd have to run it by Mr. Bennet too—but I was wondering if maybe I could play a song on my guitar to open each class. With lyrics —

we could all sing-along. Just something to set the mood. They're in school all day, and then they walk here, and some of them goofed around on the way. I think a song would help them get into the spirit of what they're going to hear."

"Ah, you are creative — just like your father! I think that's a fine idea. I guess I'll know what Mr. Bennet has to say about it when I see you next week, toting your guitar!"

Chapter 4: Death as the Less Terrible Alternative

"Do not weep for those who have found Death's embrace early, for they weep for us that linger on in this mortal world of pain."

Stewart Stafford

The Grandfather grinned as he looked out of the window on the next day the class was to visit him. Juan was in the lead, and sure enough, he had a guitar with him. What was more, a girl student walking next to Juan was carrying a violin case.

This was going to be interesting!

By now, it seemed a familiar routine was beginning to set in. The Grandfather greeted the students at the door and welcomed them into his home, where an array of teas, coffee, and treats awaited them. He was pleased to see that some of the students smiled and waved at him in a friendly way as they approached. They were beginning to feel at ease with him.

"Who is our violinist, Juan?' the Grandfather asked.

"This is Chrissy," said Juan, gesturing gallantly toward the girl as the Grandfather nodded to her and then shook Mr. Bennet's hand in welcome.

As the students settled down with their cups and desserts, Juan and Chrissy stood in front of them in the cleared space the Grandfather occupied when telling his stories. The Grandfather marveled at the transformation in Juan when the boy hefted his guitar in front of his chest and introduced the song. Gone was the shy, self-effacing young man; a shining performer had taken his place. The Grandfather remembered Juan's father telling him once that singing and playing in front of an audience was the one place on earth where he felt most confident. Juan was apparently the same way.

Slowly, Chrissy's violin began to strum on the audience's heartstrings, then build to a melancholy intensity. They could almost hear the instrument weep. Juan's singing conveyed a message of poignant hope in the face of human suffering. Some present joined in singing the chorus as it became familiar, and as the verses unfolded, more added their voices. By the last verse, almost all were joining in, and Chrissy found a way to weave a wordless instrumental ending that added sweetness and satisfaction to the moment.

The Grandfather rose, applauding and beaming his appreciation to Juan and Chrissy. Then he turned his smile on his young audience.

"Thank you, Juan and Chrissy, for setting that beautiful tone. And thank the rest of you for coming, my friends," he said. "Your coming here for this time of sharing warms my heart and encourages me to have great hope for the future. Tonight's story will let us reach out and touch a level of compassion we may not have known before. In telling it, I am reminded of the bittersweet words of author Stewart Stafford, who shared in one of his interesting stories, 'Do not weep for those who have found Death's embrace early, for they weep for us that linger on in this mortal world of pain.'"

He let that sink in for a moment, watching as the students' faces became thoughtful. Then he continued.

"For some, including the malnourished child in our story, these words seem to ring true. Life offers all of us challenges but, for some, those challenges can overwhelm. We go today once more to the Philippines. This story happened decades ago, but unfortunately, it continues to highlight a message still repeated in villages, cities, and war-torn areas throughout our world. My wish is that we all come out of the story better able to respond to those challenges.

"During the closing years of General Marcos's rule in the Philippines, many squatter's families in Manila were forcibly relocated to avoid brewing civil strife. Das Marinas, a small coastal community outside of Manila, was unprepared when an influx of new residents arrived. There were inadequate roads, schools, and bridges to handle the needs of new residents. The incoming residents also faced great challenges in finding employment and adequate sources of income.

"In 1986, the year after the relocation, the nation of the Philippines underwent a pronounced political and social transformation. A peaceful revolution, fomented by the People's Power Movement only a few months before, had toppled the long rule of General Marcos. They had installed Mrs. Cory Aquino, the widow of Senator Benigno Aquino Jr., as the nation's new president. Her husband, a popular, reform-minded, opposition leader had been assassinated a few years earlier. Now the new president set her sights on rooting out corruption and cronyism. Many who felt they lacked a voice in government were finding it a time of new hope.

"People in the Philippines are often deeply religious. It is important to know this, as our story will show. They believed that not only 'People Power' but God's power had toppled the dictator. Their pride and optimism were palpable when the international team of RYS volunteers arrived, 120 strong.

"A team of 40 of us went to Das Marinas. We came from 16 different nations and had a religious diversity among us, embracing seven religions.

"Walking down the streets of Das Marinas revealed stark levels of poverty. The faces of undernourished children were far too frequent and too emotionally moving ever to forget. The elderly with nearly toothless smiles, raggedly clothed children, and packs of terribly skinny dogs were part of the ambience on a pedestrian's journey. To better discover our community, some of us used our walks to and from work, or time during breaks, to explore different neighborhoods. We enjoyed exchanging conversations with young and old alike, lingering when time permitted.

"Within the first few days of settling into our work of building a small bridge, local people started making their way over to the worksite. Mothers stopped by. Checking on their children and at times brought us drinks. Some enjoyed talking and invited us to stop by their homes for refreshments. Friendly elementary school students had their teachers extend invitations for us to speak at their school, and a community activist brought us to speak on his radio program. It did not take long before we became a familiar but exciting part of the community. We shared in simple joys that naturally grew out of a cooperative effort to improve the community and enjoy life. Friendships grew — friendships that were planted deep in our hearts.

"While it was true that laughter was a daily occurrence at our worksite, there were some experiences that wrenched on our hearts. During the day, many children came and went from the worksite, as it was an exciting event for them to see all the unusual-looking, friendly people. It was not uncommon for participants to share their snacks with the young children who were hanging around.

"Many of us did not realize what those little snacks meant to certain children. One set of siblings started spending almost the whole day with us on a regular basis. Their rather stoic mother would visit our site on rare occasions.

"This mother had a small home near the path to the worksite. On occasion, some of us would pass and briefly exchange greetings and a few friendly words. We did not know much about her or her family's situation. Unfortunately, by the time we did, it was too late. During one conversation with other villagers, we heard that the stoic mother was desperately struggling to feed her four young children, plus her exceedingly small infant.

"Before we could communicate this news to others on our team, a neighbor reported that the mother's infant had died. We hesitatingly asked how the baby died, and the response hit us like ice water poured down our bare backs.

"Oh," he said, "the baby died of starvation!"

We were stung by the stark reality of the death of the infant. To understand and make sense of the shocking news, we began to ask questions. Pieces of information began to fit into place and present a clearer picture of the harsh realities that faced the family. The more we learned, the more unsettling it was.

The story went that the infant's father had left the family after a turbulent period. He refused to give financial or emotional support to his wife and children. The mother had spent most of her adult years raising her children and had not developed marketable skills. With no regular job or substantial way to generate income, there was not enough money to cover her family's necessities.

"The family endured periods where they had almost no food. As the situation degenerated, the mother became so desperate that when the emaciated baby cried from hunger, she fed the child moistened newspaper to dull the pain. Imagine eating newspaper!"

Some of the students shook their heads. The Grandfather saw that Chrissy's cheeks were wet with tears, and Juan's head was bowed.

"Our neighbors shared that some of the other local children that frequented our worksite were also in difficult situations and yearned for the extra attention, food, and care that our volunteers offered. We had not known.

"We drew together and went as a group to offer condolences at the wake held at the child's home. Some among our team wanted to offer prayers, some came to offer modest financial gifts. Hercule, a strong-spirited Christian from the African country of Burkina Faso, attended with a singular purpose. He aimed at resurrecting the dead infant back to life.

"Once again, I must remind you that many people in developing nations are profoundly religious. People in the Philippines believe in faith healing. It is widely practiced. Sometimes, I can say from my own experiences, what seem like medical miracles did indeed happen when people put their faith on the line. So that is the atmosphere in which this proposal was made.

"It was in the late afternoon, and we were crowded into a small, hot, simple room. Time passed, and neighbors came in and out. We were beginning to think of leaving when Hercule asked and received permission from the mother to pray over her child. Hercule, a strong faith man, remembered that he instructed his disciples to believe and inherit his spiritual authority. If he could believe, he would be able to heal the sick and raise the dead, just as Jesus had. Hercule began his prayers in anticipation of a miracle.

"The hot, crowded room seemed to fade into the background as the strong man's voice made supplications in French for this lifeless body to regain its life force. Minutes passed as he continued with undiminished intensity. The passion of his prayer flowed on.

"I won't pretend that the situation was comfortable on any level. The growing heat, the crowded room, and the surreal scene of a young man praying to give life to the corpse of an emaciated infant were almost too much for most of us. Yet brother Hercule was undaunted and continued to put his whole heart into his prayers. This impassioned young man, kneeling next to the small, thin, lifeless body, presented an unforgettable image. Some of us wondered if we in the room also needed to believe harder for this miracle to happen, but we could not. Would Hercule continue believing what seemed to be unbelievable?

"After a time, Hercule looked up and, with pleading eyes and a still confident voice, he asked the mother the painful question: "Should I continue to pray?"

There was a long, stinging silence before the mother of the child raised her head and, in a calm voice, tersely replied, "No."

The room was empty of sound during the lingering pause.

The mother spoke again, "Even if you bring my child back, what good would it do? There will still be no food to feed him."

"It was not long after the mother's response that we quietly filed out of the room. In a dark cloud of emotion, we mulled over the meaning of the mother's fatalistic response.

"Of course, many of us knew that the child could not be revived. But what the incident showed us was what a supreme tragedy it was that a mother would choose death as the preferred alternative to holding onto hope for the life of her child. This especially stung those of us who, as parents, experienced the profound happiness of holding an infant and anticipating its bright future. A gross measure of failed human responsibility seemed to be woven into this tragedy.

"The impact that this frail infant's death left on us was immeasurable. We realized that on any given day, children are dying from hunger. The events that transpired in the room drove us to question, to doubt, to reformulate our picture of life. When we left the scene of the drama, it was as if a curtain had been lifted, and we could see life from a new and deeper perspective. No longer content to simply be the audience, we wanted to rewrite the script, to be actors for change."

The Grandfather stopped speaking. Several young women were quietly sobbing. He took a long look at the faces of those gathered in front of him but also appeared to be seeing some of those from his past. He addressed those present, searching as to how to release his words without letting the full impact of their sting come too sharply.

"Each of us carries hopes and dreams within our hearts, but greater are the dreams and hopes a mother carries for her children. This is a natural and beautiful expression of what it is to be human. Disappointments can come to a parent as they see the dreams that they had for their children fall short. This happens often, but usually, it is not tragic. It is a most bitter tragedy when a loving mother is put in a situation where she finds her child's death a preferable option to the child's continued struggles in life. Such a mother's choice rips at our most essential sense of life and begs the question, 'Where is justice in this universe? Where is love?'

"The events that transpired in the room drove us to question, to doubt, to reformulate our picture of life. For some, it provided a compass that pointed us to the truly meaningful and important things in this world. Possibly for the first time, we started asking ourselves: What can we do to change the tragic cycle of poverty that so many are facing? For that is the hope of the story—that good people like yourselves will want to work to effect positive change. I hope you will want to help out in our world, for Lady Poverty has many children."

Chapter 5: To Some, Her Parts Were Worth More than Her Life

"Justice will not be served until those who are unaffected are as outraged as those who are."

Benjamin Franklin

The Grandfather was rethinking how to improve the atmosphere for telling the stories. His living room was really too small for the class to be comfortable, although they had been polite and uncomplaining about being crowded in. The Grandfather asked Mr. Bennet if the meetings should be moved to his backyard when the weather permitted. The lawn and garden provided a nice setting, and the area was comfortably large. Mr. Bennet agreed. Juan volunteered to speak to the neighbors to see if they would mind a group of teenagers gathering nearby, especially since the musical portion of the gathering was becoming more and more popular. There were several talented singers and instrumentalists among the students, and they took turns giving brief performances of music that moved the heart before the Grandfather spoke. Some young poets and writers had done short readings of their work in front of the group too. Several budding chefs had taken it upon themselves to provide tasty foods and treat for the gathering as well.

Juan thought that the best way to win the neighbors over was to invite them to come one afternoon and listen. Mr. Bennet and the Grandfather exchanged looks of pride and happiness when Juan volunteered to do the necessary public relations work. Juan was blossoming; the quiet, sorrowful young man who had lost his father was now someone walking in his father's footsteps of volunteerism. He was clearly beginning to enjoy life again and to heal somewhat from his great loss.

The next class day fell on a fine, breezy, beautiful day, and several sets of neighbors attended. To everyone's delight, they did not come empty-handed. They brought homemade baked goods and vegetable snacks with dressings.

"Good afternoon," the Grandfather began after the music and snacks had created a festive, communal atmosphere. "Benjamin Franklin, a prominent American scientist, diplomat, and philosopher, said, 'Justice will not be served until those who are unaffected are as outraged as those who are.' These words highlight why it is important to understand the situations of others. While most of us have never lived in deep poverty, squalor, or in areas where everyday violence occurs, our human inter-connectedness remains.

"From my perspective, when we recognize that we share the privilege of being one extended family, all born as an expression of the Original Parent's love, we become better equipped to respond to injustice. These are not just people in another part of the world. They are our brothers and sisters."

The Grandfather took a deep breath.

"Honduras is a beautiful country. Her green countryside is blanketed with varieties of trees and vegetation. She has beautiful coasts with clear, warm water that invites you for a swim. Her people prefer to wear smiles on their faces. The capital city, Tegucigalpa, was wisely built in the mountains to avoid the sticky, wet sauna of the lowlands' tropical heat. Poorer than most of the nations of Central America, though, many of her citizens live on the margins. Yes, Lady Poverty has set up her malign residence in this beautiful gem of a country.

"The Mayan people are the root of the culture of Honduras, with multiple dialects still being heard in homes and villages. Yet, Spanish and Hispanic influence are the dominant forces in language, culture, politics, economy, and social power. The Mayan influence runs through the blood lineage of many in this mixing lab of human relationships. Yet, the blood of the original owners of this fair land is often valued less than that of the European line.

"You may not want to hear the stories I have to share about Honduras and life in the streets. They are as bitter as bitter can be. Please do not think less of this fair land and her noble people because of these stories. It is Lady Poverty that is at fault in Honduras.

"On one of my early visits to Honduras, I came with a group of American teenagers. Conversations among them back home were often about sports, shopping, and being cool. Things like having clean drinking water, clean clothes, a safe place to sleep, the warmth of a parent, and having enough to eat were not their concerns. Those concerns, in fact, were foreign to most of them. The trip to Honduras would serve as a wake-up call to what so many people in our world are enduring.

"We were shown these realities by a dynamic social activist, Mrs. Alvarez. The day we visited Mrs. Alvarez's office, this patient, compassionate woman took time to share with us that Honduras has thousands of street children, most having been abandoned by their parents and left to fend for themselves. She then offered a rhetorical question, 'Who can protect these children if the family fails them? How can a government assist them or provide them with the parental love and care they desperately need?'

"The motherly heart of Mrs. Alvarez was toughened by more than a decade of experience working with street children. She frankly shared with us that these children are both victims and perpetrators of violence. They are not beautifully benign wildflowers or cherubs in disguise. They rob and rob often; they block the entrances of shops and harass others. Yet, they are children, and like all children, they deserve love and care. They need to experience the love of God through the touch of another. Who indeed is going to protect, guide, and care for them?

"Mrs. Alvarez's stories about the lives of street children were given a face one morning on a visit downtown. On foot, we went to the central square of the capital and visited some of the historic sites. One of our younger participants was eating a mango: a nice, sweet treat. Once he finished the mango, Sol threw the peel on the sidewalk, and a young child walking behind picked it up.

"One volunteer called out, 'Hey, you shouldn't be littering, Sol. Look, that kid has to clean up after you.'

"Sol turned around, and to his surprise, the child had the peel in his hand and was not throwing it out—he was hungrily sucking on its remains.

"This short experience served to wake us up to the sad reality that one young man's trash could provide a street child's snack. Soon after, a similar cultural shock followed.

"It was mealtime and a sunny day, so our group chose to walk downtown to find a nice outdoor restaurant and eat lunch. We enjoyed the time of eating and sharing, but when it started to look like we would finish, a group of younger children slowly neared our tables. They were eyeing the partially eaten chicken bones on our plates. As we rose to depart, the children advanced to the abandoned plates and began to pull, chew, and gnaw whatever meager meat remained on the bones.

"The daily situation in Tegucigalpa is replicated in cities throughout the world. There are many places where someone's garbage becomes a hungry child's meal.

How much longer will such scenes exist? Will our children tell the same stories to their children? Will I be able to change this story for some child? Will I model the change needed to create a more just world? These are questions we in more fortunate circumstances must ask ourselves.

"Mrs. Alvarez's work with children involved developing good levels of cooperation between government personnel and various NGOs (nongovernmental organizations). This required patient, strong, effective, and caring efforts, and she was blessed with the gifts to effect it. She didn't share with teenagers from other countries often, but she thought it was valuable in giving us a better understanding of the people's lives in her country.

"In Mrs. Alvarez's office, there was a situation board at eye level. It had rows of pictures containing the faces of lost and missing children. Although numerous, those pictures represented only a portion of those missing, as many absences are never reported. These children typically came from extremely poor families, so they were not targeted in order to get ransom money. No, some of the missing children were taken for a much more devious purpose.

"People steal a fancy car for its parts because it is worth more ripped apart into pieces and sold piece by piece. A lucrative worldwide demand for healthy human organs exists. Illicit suppliers disregard morality and operate solely out of sheer profit motives. Children are stolen from the streets for their body parts. Their organs are sold for more money than the children could ever earn in their lifetimes.

"On the day of our visit, Mrs. Alvarez had new information concerning Nina, a recently reported missing girl. In our limited time together, she addressed our group and provided insights concerning the possible fate of Nina and other missing children. While sitting in front of the situation board, those children seemed to be looking right at us. Nina's face was in a prominent place on the board as her case was active.

"Mrs. Alvarez offered us a clearer picture of the missing children. While children living on the street often suffer from the pangs of hunger, many manage to scrounge enough food so as to be healthy enough to maintain functioning bodies, parts of which can be harvested for the black market. Children are snatched or lured off the streets, and inhuman 'doctors' surgically remove their vital organs. These organs are regarded as products to these merchants of death.

"When it is a matter of life and death for those in need of an organ transplant, the person dying or their family members may be much more anxious to receive the organ than to know its origins.

"As I said, Lady Poverty has many children. She doesn't take care of them, and the world doesn't value them much. Poor children can work until they grow to be bent-to-the-ground old people and never earn the money their two kidneys can command on the black market of harvested organs. Economically speaking, a child was worth more in pieces than as a whole person, worth more dead than alive. This is a terrible reality in many places.

"Our young volunteers were moved to a different level of understanding than that of the sheltered, more carefree world they had known. They could begin to feel the pain one street child might feel when losing a young sister to a fate like this, for example. They shared a sense of the incredible tragedy of life being given so little value.

"Lady Poverty uses a razor to carve her horrors on the human souls who are caught in her snares. Sometimes she uses a knife on their bodies.

"We realized that Mrs. Alvarez was a great heroine. She was not the ordinary-appearing person she appeared to be. Her life was dedicated and meaningful, a life to be admired, a life lived to save other lives.

"While she was sharing with us her worries and broad concerns about the street children of Honduras, one of the workers from the social agency pulled her aside and shared some special good news. Nina had been located, and she was reported to be in good health. Mrs. Alvarez was ecstatic, joy exploding from her face, and expressing itself in her whole being.

"We, too, were relieved for Nina's sake. In the world of dangers that awaited many of Lady Poverty's children—the world of the lost, the abandoned, the stolen, and the disenfranchised—Nina had escaped. This time.

"Our appreciation of those things we had taken for granted grew. We looked at the everyday things we had at home—safety not being the least of them—with a little more appreciation. For those of us who came from a world of homes that always had food and shelter and a certain level of love and support, we now realized that Nina's world also existed. Knowing about it, we also knew that we shared a sense of responsibility to try to make Nina's world a little better.

"Let us, who are unaffected by these things, be as passionate to change these injustices as the hearts of those who experience them personally. Thank you for your time," the Grandfather concluded.

Figure 1: Volunteers help in Honduras

Chapter 6: Malaria Bites

"Poverty is the worst form of violence."
Mohandas K. Gandhi

In spite of the solemnity of the stories told, Juan found himself looking forward to Civics class at the Grandfather's. For one thing, he found rays of hope in the stories. If only good people would offer a hand, things could be changed for the better. For another, his school day on this particular day had been filled with challenges. He'd had a testy verbal exchange in the hallway, a tough academic test, and three hours of other classes where most things seemed boring and pointless. He was all too happy to escape to the Grandfather's.

Now that neighbors were taking part, the gatherings at the Grandfather's house, especially when they were in his backyard, seemed like picnics. More and more people were bringing food, musical instruments, song sheets, and engaging stories of their own. The smells of the flowers and hedges, the beaming sunshine and breezes, with greenery all around, the white tablecloths some of the neighbor women had set up on collapsible tables made it all seem very wonderful.

Even Mr. Bennet looked younger and happier when the class was at the Grandfather's place — and Juan was sure that, like him, Mr. Bennet felt some of his own personal cares melted away in caring about others who were less fortunate.

The Grandfather's neighbors to the right were actually sponsoring a child from Honduras now. They had researched a responsible charity, and their monthly donations fed, clothed, and housed the child and helped him stay in school. With an almost parental pride, they showed around the photos of him they had received and a letter he had penned to them.

"One less child on the streets," they said, like a mantra of hope. They were urging members of their church to take on children as well. "One less child for Lady Poverty to claim!"

The Grandfather was obviously exceedingly pleased by it all. Sometimes, Juan saw him closing his eyes during the music as if watching a beautiful dream. Juan found himself relaxing after the stress of his day, basking in the joy of making music with Chrissy, the ambience of the garden, and the gentle murmurs of the guests and breezes.

He was taking a bow to applause after he and Chrissy had finished their musical piece when:

"Ouch!" A person in the front row slapped his own neck. "Sorry! Mosquito!" he said. "I hate those things!"

Everyone laughed.

The Grandfather rose, and following Juan's introduction, he asked those gathered: "Have any of you had malaria? Do you have friends or family members that have had that wicked disease? No one? Well, that is a good thing. I don't think you will get malaria from that bite, but if you were somewhere else in the world, you very well might. There are about 230 million cases of malaria each year, and almost half a million people die of it, mostly Lady Poverty's children. In fact, the diseases of malaria and poverty go hand in hand. Malaria drains poor countries' economies, making them more vulnerable to the disease. Then the disease creates a further drain on resources. Yes, malaria walks hand-in-hand with Lady Poverty and stalks her children.

"There are only a couple of thousand cases of malaria in the United States per year, and most of them are in people who have traveled back from countries where the disease is prevalent, like sub-Saharan Africa and South Asia. I will share my personal experience with malaria and try to give a sense of how this disease impacts so many people's lives in Africa.

"When I think back to my time in Uganda, it is mostly fine memories that come to mind. A smile draws across my face as I reflect on the resilient people, the beauty of the countryside, the lively religious spirit, and its promise of a brighter future. Filtering through those thoughts, one troubling memory lingers in both my mind and body: the memory of malaria.

"Growing up in New York City, malaria seemed so distant, so intangible. I first heard about malaria in school when Mr. Mauro, my science teacher, showed our half-attentive class newsreels about tropical diseases. Many of the images focused on situations in distant Africa. These were hard-to-watch images because they often concentrated on sick children. Having a personal experience with the disease never entered my mind. Yet, over time, I have grown to understand that life has a way of offering us the unexpected.

"Malaria became a personal matter for me and seven members of our Religious Youth Service (RYS) team in the Lira District of Uganda. Out of 30 participants, our little group was selected by mosquitoes infected with malarial parasites in an indiscriminate internationalist spirit! The seven infected were from Kenya, Ethiopia, Italy, and the USA. Each of us found our bodies wracked with high fevers, sweats, and chills, along with the soreness and pain that accompany the disease.

"My initial bout with the disease was tough, and I spent a week recovering in Clara Maass Hospital in New Jersey on returning home. Some of the seven infected team members took longer to recover. While years have passed since my initial outbreak, the disease still delivers personal reminders. On occasion, I break out in night sweats and awaken in the morning in a soaked garments — a small price to pay when you realize that so many children who get the disease never recover.

"The year I got malaria, 2008, almost a million people died of it, nearly 90% of the deaths occurring in

Africa. In the Lira District of Uganda, where we worked, malaria killed nearly 25% of the children before they reached the age of five.

"In the middle of the last century, in many areas, malaria seemed well on its way toward complete eradication. Then a dramatic increase occurred when the pesticide DDT was banned in many nations. While DDT effectively kills mosquitoes, it also has a very detrimental impact on other aspects of the environment. However, the ban on DDT in recent decades has become more controversial. As with many issues, the debate over the banning of DDT has been strongly influenced by politics which, in turn, is directly impacted by financial considerations. From my own perspective, the central focus should be on the question: How can we most efficiently work to protect human lives, especially the children, who are most vulnerable? Malaria should not be the killer it currently is.

"Some local medical personnel in Uganda told us that the strain of malaria we received in the Lira District was especially potent. As a strong adult with access to medicine and the care of a good hospital, it still took a great deal of energy to keep my ship afloat. How much harder must it be for undernourished infants, toddlers, and children of families who have little or no access to medical care? One out of four children in Lira dies by the time he or she is five. This fact deserves repeating because it is true not only in Lira but also in many other communities throughout tropical Africa.

"Lady Poverty does not love her children. She kills them with violence and virulence that we in the developed world do not know. As Gandhi said, 'Poverty is the worst form of violence,' because poverty snuffs out the hopes, and often times, the very lives of so many of the world's children.

"In some ways, I may say I am honored to have shared this disease with Lady Poverty's children. I gained a taste of their suffering from it—just a taste—and it made me want to help them more."

Juan hung his head in shame as the Grandfather wrapped up his story. What right had he, he wondered, to complain about a "bad" day in which he had still had plenty to eat and drink, fresh, new clothes to wear, a home to go back to at night, medical care if he needed it, a mother who loved him, and a father who had left him a legacy of service? He had never known Lady Poverty or the horrific effects she wrought on her children. From now on, he vowed, he would be more grateful for what he had and be more proactive in serving those who had less.

Seeing the Grandfather smiling at him whimsically, Juan had a feeling the elderly gentleman had read his thoughts.

Chapter 7: From Scavengers to Prize Winners

"Overcoming poverty is not a gesture of charity. It is the protection of a fundamental human right: the right to dignity and a decent life."
Nelson Mandela

A spell of bad weather had hit the town, and going to the Grandfather's yard and the garden was obviously going to be impossible. Yet, with the neighbors and others starting to come to the Grandfather's house each week, there was certainly not enough room in the Grandfather's rather compact house.

The solution seemed to be that, rather than go to the Grandfather, they needed to bring the Grandfather to them.

Kyle was one of Mr. Bennet's students who had already passed his driver's test and had a license. With some trepidation, Mr. Bennet handed Kyle the keys to his own car. He then turned to Juan.

"Maybe you can ride shotgun, Juan," he instructed him. "I'd feel better lending my car if I knew there were two pairs of eyes in the front seat! Chrissy should go along too. She can sit with the Grandfather in the back seat."

"You've got nothing to worry about," Kyle assured the teacher. "I passed my test with flying colors!"

"Well, don't try flying around in my car. Remember, you are going to have an elderly man on board, and you need to be mindful of his nerves and stamina."

Once he had been delivered to the school safely, the Grandfather walked down the hallway, looking around to get his bearings. Students from other classes stared at him at first, shrugged, and then looked away. Juan was proud of the Grandfather—he walked straight and was well-dressed. In spite of being in a strange place, he looked like he could handle himself in the situation. In fact, he could have been mistaken for a retired teacher or superintendent. Juan gently steered him to Mr. Bennet's classroom.

The Grandfather's eyes lit up when he saw all the young people he recognized sitting in their seats in the classroom. On impulse, the class rose respectfully to greet him, applauding, with some even hugging him. A young person grasped hold of each of his hands and guided him to a seat next to Mr. Bennet's desk.

"May I get you anything?" Mr. Bennet asked. "A coffee—or some tasty snack?"

"Coffee, yes, thank you," said the Grandfather.

"It's teacher's lounge coffee," warned Mr. Bennet. "Nothing like that Guatemalan confection you serve us!"

"'Twill do. 'Twill serve," said the Grandfather.

One of the students called out: "That's Shakespeare! Romeo and Juliet! When Mercutio gets stabbed!"

"Very good," said the Grandfather, impressed. "You must be studying Shakespeare in English class."

With a warning glance to the students to behave themselves in his absence, Mr. Bennet went out to get coffee for the Grandfather.

"This is different from our usual digs, isn't it?" the Grandfather asked. "But it's a good setting for my story because today's tale involves a very special school—and a very special class of young ladies."

The students settled down to listen as Mr. Bennet returned and discreetly put the cup of coffee within the Grandfather's reach before sitting down himself.

"One of our great RYS volunteers, Father Nithiya, was in Madurai, India, when he contacted me. I'll tell you more about Fr. Nithiya in another story. In India, he helped organize mobile medical teams that traveled into the countryside and performed eye operations for the poor. These teams were literally giving the blind a chance to see."

He paused for a moment as the students nodded in recognition of this good service.

"Fr. Nithiya shared about an upcoming Peace Festival that he was helping to build a coalition of support for. The Gandhi Museum and a wide variety of local organizations had agreed to help assist and sponsor various parts of the festival. The week-long Peace Festival offered programs that would involve school children throughout the city of Madurai. The festival's busy schedule included drama events, music, sports competitions, games, essay contests, spiritual talks, service projects, and a large parade of marching bands. Father Nithiya encouraged RYS to follow up the festival with a service project. We wrote back our agreement.

"When we arrived in Madurai after a long journey, it was extremely exciting to see the involvement of thousands of students in the festival programs. Even though the preparations for the upcoming RYS service project kept us busy, we did manage to enjoy opportunities to observe some of the festival events. At one event, Mr. Pande, the director of the Gandhi Museum, pointed out a certain group of children wearing blue school uniforms.

"He told us, 'Those girls are from the school where RYS volunteers will be helping. They have been raised in families who work and live in the local garbage dump, but now things can be different for them.'

"Yes, my friends, there are people in the world so stricken by Lady Poverty that they live in the garbage dumps of cities, looking for scraps to eat or sell. In parts of the world, garbage provides a meager sub-subsistence income that barely keeps the human 'scavengers' alive.

"In India, the situation for those collecting garbage is made worse by the social and religious taboos that stigmatize them, keeping them down. Collecting garbage often becomes a family's destiny: grandparents, parents, children, and their descendants are compelled across generations to spend their lives scavenging through garbage. Lady Poverty doesn't like to enslave just a few people in one generation. Poverty is very often cyclical, passing from generation to generation to generation.

"Socially and religiously segregated, these families are part of a larger group known by a variety of names. To some, they are known as 'Dalits — the lowest caste among all classes. Some are branded as Untouchables. The government labels them the 'Scheduled Class.'

"Gandhi preferred the term 'Harijan because it meant 'Children of God.'

"At the Peace Festival, there was a group of children dressed neatly in blue uniforms. They were

94

anxiously observing the activities from a little distance. These children were from families who were among the ragged who lived and worked their daylight hours picking through large piles of garbage at the city's dump. As children, they were familiar with putrid smells, rancid debris, and toxic waste. Necessity forced them to search for something that they could sell to earn them a much-needed meal.

"The young girls in the blue uniforms had known so little of childhood things before they went to the school. Instead of the fresh smells of flowers, regular meals, activities, and games, they faced daily the crushing weight of hunger and family poverty. The only playing fields they knew were the sides of mounds of garbage. Their known world was entrapped in a permanent stench, adding to the social stigma surrounding them. To rise above it, all was a dream that many of them could barely imagine.

"Through the donations and efforts of the Gandhi Museum and local Gandhi affiliates, a modest school had been launched to serve a number of girls who had previously been scavenging. The school included several finished and some unfinished classrooms. The RYS volunteers had determined to help finish some of the classrooms.

"At the school, teachers provided both academic and job training to prepare the girls to claim brighter futures. One special part of their training brought them boundless joy — the classes in traditional Indian dance. The students relished the dance classes as an opportunity to train extremely hard, and those that excelled were selected to perform at the Peace Festival. For the students, this was going to be their first public appearance, and they were very excited and nervous about performing for a large audience.

"As an observer at the Peace Festival, I watched as the girls from our school went through their final dance preparations. It was important for me to understand something of the journey the girls had made to reach this event. When they walked past us, our eyes were glued to their beautiful but nervous faces. The girls gracefully walked on by and onto the stage to make their dance offering. Dressed brightly in simple, pleasing costumes, they moved fluidly to the complex rhythms of the traditional music.

"Traditional Indian music is a physical expression of deep spirituality. To perform the dance, the dancer needs to become one with the music, entering a realm where the dancer is the music. The lean, dark-skinned, graceful girls, smiling with their eyes, spoke beautifully through their motions. They had mastered an inspirational language of dance as they moved across the stage.

"As an eyewitness, it was clear that these were moments of liberation for them. Their movements revealed the essence of who they were—God's children, dancers, owners of this moment in time. It was pure beauty as we watched them express something timeless through dance: the worth and beauty of a human being, no matter how destitute, no matter how desperate the person's situation. All they had needed was a chance.

"I was reminded of a quote by Nelson Mandela, who said, 'Overcoming poverty is not a gesture of charity. It is the protection of a fundamental human right: the right to dignity and a decent life.'

"More than a dozen groups danced that morning for the large audience of children, parents, and spectators. Following the performances, a highly anticipated closing awards ceremony was held in which the top-performing groups would receive awards. As the crowd of spectators pushed closer to the stage in anticipation of hearing the contest results, 'our' girls huddled together anxiously, awaiting the decision of the judges.

"Observing the girls, one could read an apprehensive hope and anticipation on their faces. You could imagine their painful self-doubt and self-questioning: 'Could we really win? Could we ever be good enough?' The announcement of the winners created a scene of perfect joy. The young girls, daughters of garbage scavengers, smiled with their body language as well as their faces when they heard the good news.

"They began jumping up and down as they shouted in Tamil, 'We won, we won, we did it!'

"Displaying a newly earned sense of confidence, the young ladies walked onto the stage to receive their well-deserved awards. They collectively took a bow and heard the audience's thunderous applause. Such recognition and appreciation freed them from the deadening gravity of social circumstance. The sounds and sights of this event lifted their spirits far above the drudgery of the past as they saw for the first time the beautiful vistas of possibility and promise.

"The lithely built schoolgirls demonstrated an internal strength that would not accept a downtrodden fate. The stigma of being labeled an outcast might conceivably have weighed their spirits down to a compliant acceptance. It had done so to countless people throughout generations. However, given a chance by an outstretched hand of caring, the girls worked hard to show to themselves and others that they had something special to offer.

"Surely, the bright smiles on their faces at the awards ceremony would not remain indefinitely, but the positive experience that they shared would stay forever in their hearts.

"A few months after the conclusion of the successful Peace Festival and an exciting RYS project in Madurai, Fr. Nithiya had an opportunity to meet and share with Mother Teresa. During their conversation, Fr. Nithiya spoke about his RYS experiences in Hungary and in India. On hearing about those cooperative efforts, Mother Teresa wrote the following note of encouragement and guidance to the RYS team.

'To the RYS India Participants (Mother Teresa):

I will pray for God's blessing on your beautiful work of love.

Do it for the glory of God and the good of the people.'

"These few words of Mother Teresa touched our hearts and were in accord with Fr. Nithiya's mentors, St. Francis and Mahatma Gandhi. To do beautiful works of love for the glory of God and the good of people is a divine mandate and a heavenly call to action for all who have ears to listen and the heart to serve."

Mr. Bennet rose to his feet, applauding with all the others. Juan felt as if they were not only clapping for the Grandfather's story — they, too, were clapping for the courageous young school girls who stood up to show the world what bravery, beauty, and accomplishment looked like, even from among the lowliest on the social ladder. Kyle placed his fingers in his mouth to make a loud, piercing whistle, and others began pounding on their desks and stomping their feet in a spontaneous expression of "Bravo!"

After a few minutes, Mr. Bennet signaled for the students to quiet down.

"I think they might be able to hear you in India," he smiled.

Chrissy, blinking back tears, said stoutly, "I hope they do!"

And the applause, stomping, and whistling broke out again for the courageous young girls of India.

Chapter 8: The Starting Place

"Home is where one starts from."

T. S. Eliot

Since the Grandfather had come to them that particular day, extra class time was usually taken up getting to and from the elderly gentleman's home. Mr. Bennet suggested that the Grandfather tell them another story.

"Yes," the Grandfather said, although he looked a little tired. He sipped coffee for a few minutes and then seemed to brace himself for another monologue.

"The great poet, T.S. Eliot, once penned, 'Home is where one starts from.' Our story will be one where a family starts a new life in a new home. I hope you enjoy it.

"More than a decade has passed since the Religious Youth Service (RYS) did an overly ambitious service project in the Republic of Trinidad and Tobago. Many of the 70 participants were around 16 years old, just your ages. Often, they dealt with things and acted in ways fitting their age. I can say it was somewhat like the way Kyle drives."

The class laughed while Mr. Bennet looked concerned.

"Kyle!" he said. "Did you speed while driving the Grandfather here?"

Chrissy said, "He did drive too fast."

Juan said, "There was that stop sign he missed—"

Mr. Bennet's brows were knit in a frown. He looked like a pot coming to a boil and ready to spill over.

The Grandfather raised his hand.

"Now, now, John," he said to Mr. Bennet, and the class gaped at hearing the teacher called by his first name. "I haven't been to all the places I've been and seen all I've seen to be worried about an exuberant young man behind the wheel on some quiet suburban streets! Kyle did all right."

Chrissy shrugged. "Yes, he did all right. Just."

"He was okay," said Juan. "We're here, after all."

"Hm," said Mr. Bennet. He looked disgruntled but satisfied.

"The young people in the RYS project were drawn from seven nations," said the Grandfather. "They slept in tents, struggled with water shortages, adolescent angst, tropical heat, and a multitude of challenges during this, their first cross-cultural experience.

"Fortunately, we were blessed to have good working partners in the Rose Foundation and in Habitat for Humanity. These outstanding organizations helped us find ways to make our three weeks' investment a worthwhile experience for the young volunteers and the families and communities we worked with.

"Since the early days of its settlement, Trinidad and Tobago have been a multiracial society. People from various backgrounds have worked, shared, and created families together. With the passing of generations, lineages have mixed and melted, creating many hues within the country's faces.

"Unlike numerous societies where various ethnic

groups live parallel but separate lives, those in Trinidad and Tobago have digested aspects of each other's cultures and found a way to add their own unique touch. The national foods offer a good example of this, with dishes that originally came from India and Africa that have assimilated 'Trini' flavoring and now feature their own unique tastes.

"Although the islands of Trinidad and Tobago are not large, they do exhibit an unusually broad diversity of religious expression. Christianity holds the allegiance of a large segment of the population and is expressed in various forms. Yet half the islands' population has roots in the Indian subcontinent, so Hinduism and Islam play a large role in shaping the spirit of the people too. Chinese religions, the Rastafarians, and other groups also have adherents, while remnants of Native American spirituality persist.

"With warm and friendly people, Trinidad and Tobago were an attractive host for the project. As young ambassadors representing their respective religions and nations, the volunteers worked and lived side by side with those in the local community and with each other.

"We scheduled our arrival to coincide with the launch of a project hosted by Habitat for Humanity — The National Leaders Build. The Build was designed to bring public awareness to the shortage of suitable housing for low-income families.

"On the opening day of The Build, media and spectators crowded around a makeshift stage under a protective canopy that shielded us from both rain and direct sun. Preceding the formal start of the work, several speeches were offered, including remarks from the nation's president and the leader of the opposition party. The media were present to cover the events. When these speeches and snacks were finished, the construction commenced. We were under the supervision of skilled professionals working as volunteers with Habitat for Humanity, an international organization built on Christian principles that take to heart Jesus's mandate to care for the least of his children. The organization carries out this mandate by building homes for poor families in need of proper shelter.

"For most, it is the first home they have ever owned, and it comes with the pride of ownership and the sense of settling into a community.

"Building homes for families trying to get a step ahead in life was a challenge. Yet, despite the heat and lack of professional building skills, we poured ourselves into all aspects of the work during our work week. We carried bricks, moved soil and lumber, mixed cement, and landscaped the grounds.

"On our breaks, we walked around and talked with neighbors, learning much about the people who lived in the community and especially about the three families that would be moving into the houses we were constructing.

"For many of the international participants, walking through the poor community near the worksite was their closest experience with poverty. The dilapidated state of many of the houses, the barely clothed and unattended children, the empty pockets of unemployed men hanging around this run-down, neglected environment stood in stark contrast to the hopeful work being done to construct the Habitat homes.

"This was a poor neighborhood. Yet, it was not in the same league of misery as the sidewalk 'homes' of Mumbai, India, or the sprawling encampments of refugees prevalent in too many areas of the world — situations that seemed to conspire ruthlessly to prevent escape. In our Trinidad/Tobago community, the fate of the children did not seem so absolutely predetermined.

"There are certain raw impressions of poverty that linger indelibly in my mind—the skinny, 'Untouchable' children living off the proceeds from the garbage they collect; the helpless eyes of a mother in a refugee camp who has lost her family, friends, and home; the sight and smells of a Punjab railroad station late at night with hundreds of families sleeping on a crowded cement floor. Traveling along the rails in India, you can still see tens of thousands who have laid out cardboard alongside the tracks, staking a claim to residency.

"There is an unrelenting force in poverty that is much like a gravitational pull. Imagine trying to walk on Jupiter or someplace where the gravity is five times, ten times, or a hundred times stronger than on our home planet. That is what it must be like for a child trying to escape the gravity of poverty in certain parts of our world.

The irresistible force is simply too strong for many human beings. It is my sense that this gravitational burden will only shift or overcome in proportion to the degree we remember that we are our brothers' and sisters' keepers.

"On the second day of The Build, the president, the opposition party leader, and the religious and civic leaders who had gathered the day before were gone. The press and TV crews that had snapped pictures and filmed interviews had left as well.

"This became a time when our sense of personal responsibility grew. Our sense of personal responsibility helped us work through differences in cultural perspectives as well as to weather the heat and rain so typical on a tropical isle.

"The environment at the worksite and in the community took on the comfortable feeling of our belonging to an extended family with each member having a unique value and role.

"In the joint effort to realize our common purpose, time passed quickly. We officially took part in the closing of The Build on a Thursday but, after the ceremony, we felt we had some finishing touches that needed to be done, so we returned the following day.

"Our unexpected visit surprised the neighbors. Casually, parents and children approached members of the team and shared their feelings.

"One mother shared, 'We can believe that God has a plan for us because we felt God's love and care with the way you cared for and played with our children. We don't feel abandoned because you have shown that people really do care.'

"We visited the new homes to present the new homeowners with flowers and a small housewarming gift. This small offering opened the heart of one father, and he pulled me aside to share his feelings.

'When you arrived, my wife and I were at a point of giving up on our marriage. I did not think it was worth trying anymore. No one outside our family really cared if we made it or not. We were told they were going to build a house for us, and that was hard to believe. When we saw all the people coming to help, it moved us. This changed something in my heart.

'You people wanted our house to be filled with a family; the volunteers wanted it to be home. My wife and I talked at night when the people left, and we began to share some dreams together. This was the first time in a long time that we could really begin to imagine things being better together. Last night, when we were talking, we joked that once the house was built, no one would care anymore. But today you came with the flowers, and that really convinced us that people do care. My wife and I care, we care about our child, and we are going to make this house a home.'

"This father shared with us the deepest meaning of service. We had thought our service work was to help build a house, but that was only a small part of what we were doing.

"We were building a home for the sake of love. In the end, that is what service is all about: love. When you feel love for and from people, you have never met before, but whom you have served, you understand that a peaceful, prosperous, happy world truly is possible. All it takes to banish Lady Poverty from our earth is active love for our fellow human beings."

The Grandfather smiled and said, "Kyle, will you show me some love now by driving me home? Two stories in one day have tired me out."

"Sure," said Kyle, rising. Juan and Chrissy also rose to accompany the Grandfather to his home.

"Show some love for the speed limit while you are at it, Kyle," said Mr. Bennet, and everyone, including the Grandfather, laughed.

Part III: War, Natural Disasters, and Civil Strife

Chapter 9: Tragedy and Revival in Honduras

"Storms draw something out of us that calm seas don't."
Reverend Bill Hybels

When asked earlier in the semester whether they had any ideas about local service projects, the class had come up with very usual suggestions. Now, they were popping with ideas to explore their community and its needs. Mr. Bennet had broken them into small "idea" groups to design proposed projects for the whole class to consider.

Chrissy, Juan, and Kyle were one small group. Chrissy and Juan tended to hang out together anyway, planning the music for each class, so it seemed natural to gravitate toward one another as part of a small planning group. Kyle played a mean digital keyboard, so he was interested in being part of a trio with them.

As the three arrived at the Grandfather's house together, they were not talking about music. They were strenuously sharing differing understandings of certain philosophical questions.

"There can't be a God," said Kyle. "Or, if there is, He's not such a nice guy. I mean, if God is a God of love, how come there's so much suffering and evil in the world? Is that all part of some master plan?"

"I agree with you that doesn't sound like a very merciful God to make a plan like that!" said Chrissy, shuddering. "Children dodging people who want to kill them for their body parts? Children scavenging through garbage dumps just to put together a meal? Mothers hoping their children stay dead, so they don't have to suffer anymore? That is not a God plan!"

Juan said, "I think it's us humans who bring so much trouble, violence, and confusion into the world. We have personal responsibilities that not even God can interrupt. Each of us has ways to make the world better or to make it worse. People aren't suffering from Lady Poverty because there isn't enough in the world—it's because not enough good people are working together to get them the help they need. And there are some people who profit off the poor people's misery, like those body parts harvesters."

"Okay, I can buy that," said Kyle. "Human responsibility. But what about natural disasters and things like that? Sometimes those are called 'acts of God'! Are they, do you think?"

"No," said Juan. "It could be that our human interference with nature causes natural disasters or our lack of planning for them. I don't believe those are acts of God. Again, I think it's human responsibility. The good thing is, most of the time, when natural disasters happen, lots of people all over the world pitch in money and time to help. To me, those are the acts of God."

They were at the house now, and the Grandfather stepped out to greet them and all the other students.

As they shuffled into his home, he announced, "Today, we will be sharing about the tragedy through a natural disaster and the revival and power that comes with working together to solve problems after such devastating events."

"He must be a mind reader," Juan murmured to Chrissy. "It sounds like he knew what we were talking about!"

Kyle was going to do a solo today on the keyboard he had carried with him. Juan and Chrissy were relieved because they had a test in another class the next day and had little time preparing a musical offering.

In his usual, almost out-of-control way, Kyle played a powerful song that he had said was of his own composition. The crashes of the chords sounded like wind and waves, thunder, and cracks of lightning. The Grandfather's small house seemed to rock. After stunning them with the power of his flashing fingers on the keyboard, in the end, Kyle did a spine-chilling crescendo that left them all gaping before they broke into hesitant applause.

"Why, thank you, Kyle," said the Grandfather as Kyle put away his keyboard. "I admire your energy. Your, ah, musical number was more appropriate than you know because today's story is about a hurricane — Hurricane Mitch. Your music reminds me of words from the author Bill Hybels who shares this about human nature: 'Storms draw something out of us that calm seas don't.' And, I will say, you certainly played up a storm.

"Is anybody here originally from Honduras? A couple; that is good. I will be sharing tonight a story about one of the most challenging times in Honduras's recent history. The story will let us explore and gain insight into the resiliency of the people and how they responded to the crisis.

"Hurricane Mitch packed a punch when it hit Central America. Mitch struck Honduras with heavy winds and dropped a record 75 inches of torrential rains in parts of the countryside. The storm's November 1998 departure left behind an epic trail of destruction at a time when the hurricane season had officially been declared finished. In Honduras, over 11,000 men, women, and children perished or disappeared because of the ravaging storm.

"Months later, 40 RYS volunteers from 15 nations arrived in the capital city of Tegucigalpa. During the following weeks of service, the media regularly covered the story, presenting to the public images of young Honduran and international volunteers working side by side. The cooperative efforts of the volunteers served as a source of encouragement to a nation deep in the process of healing and rebuilding.

"After the wrath of Mitch, large, steel structures that were once the bridges of Honduras stood bent, broken, and sunk into submission. Washed away were thousands of small shacks built on the hilly terrain overlooking normally tame rivers. Relentless rains weakened the foundations of houses, while mudslides indiscriminately buried homes, trapping all living creatures. Large parts of the nation's capital went underwater as rivers reached levels never imagined by city planners.

"The devastation of Hurricane Mitch and the early stages of the rebuilding efforts were part of broadcast news throughout the world, attracting volunteers from many

nations and organizations. Unfortunately, even after bodies were buried, roads cleared, and the rebuilding was well underway, many Hondurans remained in a stupor, a state of civic shock.

"Prior to Hurricane Mitch's arrival, the flood-prone Tegucigalpa neighborhood of El Sapo had a reputation for being one of the poorest and the most neglected in the city. The impact of the storm magnified existing community problems. People lost friends and family members, businesses were destroyed, jobs disappeared, and local homes and infrastructure remained heavily damaged. Many vital city services remained cut off, and residents had no clear vision or plan on how to turn things around.

"Our local project director, Mario Salinas, decided on a practical way to help residents of El Sapo. The massive and worsening problem of garbage and debris removal had become a major concern in the wake of the killer storm. The little stream that cuts through the community during the deluge had transformed into a destructive river that washed away roads, leaving large potholes that soon became filled with debris. The local and international volunteers on the RYS worked together to try to tackle the garbage problem.

"Without functional roads, garbage trucks refused to enter into parts of the El Sapo community. Garbage and refuse were being dumped in empty lots and piled up in mounds around the stream. By the time our team arrived in June, six months of garbage had accumulated into piles that were a clear public health hazard.

"The young volunteers of RYS walked through the community, evaluating the size and scope of the dirty job that lay ahead. We realized that, in addition to the physical work, we had to mentally and physically prepare ourselves to remove the tons and tons of stinky, accumulated garbage.

"Garbage has a life cycle of its own: the older it gets, the fouler and nastier it smells, making it harder to move. Freshly tossed garbage soon gets buried under succeeding piles of trash. Like a geometric progression, the number of bugs and crawling life forms multiply with age. Remove the top layer of garbage, and succeeding layers contain an active world of maggots and other insects.

Pockets of methane gas form in the lower levels of the oldest piles. By removing the garbage, the gas is released with a smell that can literally knock a person out.

"To prevent overexposure to health hazards, we planned to rotate members of our team so that some would be clearing out the garbage while others would be constructing public garbage bins. On our first day at the worksite, though, the staff decided to have everyone work together on the dirty job of cleaning up the garbage. No one was going to escape —every one of us was going to get

down and get dirty. This was a team-building challenge that would either make us or break us.

"Many squeamish volunteers hesitated to reach into refuse that smelled so awful. They delayed putting their hands and arms into the litter-filled stream to pull out slimy containers. One participant challenged a few others, and soon more competitions started. They challenged themselves for the honor of achieving the most garbage bags filled with the nastiest garbage. Soon the squeamishness disappeared and was replaced by youthful laughter as the challengers made evaluations and comparisons.

"Starting with the dirtiest job proved to be helpful in creating a team spirit. The garbage was a great equalizer, allowing us to share in the sense of accomplishment. One smiling volunteer piped up, 'We saw, we smelled, and we conquered.'

"The work was often tedious and seemingly endless. El Sapo's stream was so polluted that we pulled out numerous carcasses of decaying birds and animals daily. The momentous amount of plastic littering the area made us wonder why, as humanity, we have taken so long to switch to biodegradable containers.

"During our workday, on occasion, we would catch the sight of a community member throwing garbage in a field. This behavior added a sense of futility to our work. It became increasingly clear that no matter how hard we labored, we would not accomplish the cleanup without greater community support and especially some commitment from the government to restart garbage pickups.

"Several meetings with community leaders were arranged to discuss community commitment. Removing litter and debris needed to become everyone's priority. Success would be transitory without municipal support.

"Mr. Salinas decided to follow up on the mayor's previous offer of support by requesting that she speak to the volunteers on the project and meet with her constituents.

She agreed to come and timed the visit so that she could see the volunteers at work.

"On her arrival, the media was already actively filming the work and doing interviews. The mayor moved through a crowd that was filled with mothers, families, and young volunteers. She spoke words of encouragement and listened to the residents. With personal warmth full of genuine concern, she made a deep impression.

"Moved by what she saw and heard, the mayor announced publicly her pledge to reestablish garbage pickups in El Sapo and provide resources for the building of more garbage bins.

"The mayor's visit and her promises were proof to residents that El Sapo was no longer a forgotten community. Community pride was renewed, which inspired many to action. Growing numbers of neighbors gravitated to help with the jobs we faced.

"Children clustered around, encouraging, laughing, playing and, at times, working side by side with the volunteers. Their parents saw to it that we had enough to drink and eat. Families made us feel at home when we needed to use a toilet or rest in the shade.

"Individuals and then teams of neighborhood men joined us in the construction of the new garbage bins, while community organizations made decisions on the locations of the additional garbage pickup areas. The feeling was growing that our team was no longer considered foreign guests but, instead, contributing members of the community.

"With the enhanced cooperation between local organizations and RYS, a more realistic approach to the cleanup emerged. Education on the health risks linked to garbage and poor sanitation was begun. Upstream communities were taught the importance of clean water and the reasons for not dumping garbage into the stream.

The Sisters of Charity, a Roman Catholic Order founded by Mother Teresa, agreed to follow up on our efforts to support a 'no litter' policy for the community. The Sisters began offering health and education programs to the residents of El Sapo and its neighboring communities, a service that continued well after our departure.

"At a decisive point, something can reawaken the spirit of a devastated community. That awakening may be generated by the kindness offered through a stranger's helping hand. An awakening happened in the community of El Sapo. Thanks to the media, the story of the awakening was played out in front of the eyes of a nation looking for reasons to hope.

"So, my young friends, know that whatever service projects you choose to do, you can and will have an impact for good. I've seen many projects have a ripple effect far beyond the original starting point, like this one. You can go to sleep at night after such a service project, knowing you did your part to make the world a better place."

Kyle raised his hand and asked if he could close the session with a song. Mr. Bennet reluctantly agreed. Everyone looked a little on edge, wondering if Kyle was going to unleash another hurricane of discordance.

To their pleased surprise, Kyle's fingers tickled the keyboard tenderly. A beautiful, rippling song poured out, as hopeful as sunshine after rain. As they listened, the purity of the notes and melody seemed to promise a world where, with a little hard work and care, cleanliness and renewal could abound.

"Ah," said the Grandfather. "We have all heard of the calm before the storm.

This was the calm after the storm. Thank you, Kyle."

Chapter 10: Our Human Family

"I've learned that people will forget what you said, people will forget what you did, but people will never forget what you made them feel."

Maya Angelou

Once the weather cleared, the Grandfather's talks once more became community events. Small groups of young men and women were once again gathering in his yard and garden. Juan and Chrissy were setting the table with drinks and light snacks. Additional table space was reserved in anticipation of the extra food brought through the generosity of the neighborhood guests, some of whom were already appearing, smiling, along the Grandfather's hedges, their hands full of covered dishes and plates of treats.

Some students had brought their own musical instruments; a talented sketch artist held a pad and busily made pictures of those clustered at the site. A few poets found a place on the lawn where they could share recently crafted verses with one another.

The Grandfather was relaxed, happy, and freely mixing with the students and his neighbors. His time in near seclusion had weighed heavily on him. The gabble of all the socializing was music to his ears.

After some time, Mr. Bennet cued Juan a reminder that it was time to get started. Juan and Chrissy came forward to sing a short song. Then they put down their instruments and took their seats. The Grandfather rose.

"Warm greetings to you all!" The Grandfather said. "It is good to sense your energy and interest, for today we travel to Hungary to a settlement created for orphans.

"In the Sahih Bukhari, the Prophet Mohammad is said to have shared the following: 'I and the person who looks after the orphan and provides for him, will be in Paradise like this (putting his index finger and middle finger together).'

"These are very fitting words to begin our story, for many faiths speak of taking care of orphans.

"The RYS, 100 strong, arrived in Budapest in the early days of summer, which were invitingly warm. The sights and sounds that accompanied our international group manifested as a diversity of colors, hues, and tones. We were gathering in a historic square as representatives from 32 nations, two dozen cultures, and nine different religions. We were all willing participants in a grand experiment of service for the sake of others. We were curious about what lay ahead and excited to meet each other.

"In the summer of 1991, Hungary was in the early stages of a massive transition from a communist state to something refreshingly new. People who had been longing for change found themselves empowered with new freedoms and opportunities. A vitality and optimism filled the air as you walked through the historic center of Budapest, the public square.

"Daily, a flurry of witnessing and promotional activity, representing a wide diversity of religious, political, commercial, and social interests was taking place.

Standing on intermittent street corners were Jehovah Witnesses handing out magazines. Strolling towards pedestrians were both young Evangelicals and civic activists attempting to spark interest in their causes. On occasion, brightly robed adherents chanting praises to Krishna added color and sound to the panorama.

"Two short years earlier, police in uniform and agents in plain clothes would have swarmed out on the street to harass, intimidate, and possibly arrest anyone freely expressing their beliefs. The old government worked to create a culture of intimidation. Communist governments feared religion because it created in some a loyalty grander than that inspired by a political party. Leaders also saw danger in the unfettered free exchange of political ideas since this could undermine loyalty to Communist doctrines, challenge authority, and upset the status quo. The recent peaceful revolution was a reaction to that restrictive way of life.

"The situation in Hungary resembled that of many nations in Eastern and Central Europe where the 'Iron Curtain' had recently come down. The rapid and largely non-violent collapse of Communist governments throughout Eastern Europe opened doors to the world, and the years 1989-1996 marked a time of great transition. Streams of international volunteers and non-government agencies poured people and resources into the region. During this time, RYS contributed over 500 volunteers from every religion and over 40 nations in programs offering services to needy communities in Hungary, Poland, Czechoslovakia, Romania, Slovenia, and Croatia.

"In Hungary, we were going to work on a variety of service projects. The media saw our coming as an important story, and they spent three weeks filming a documentary that was shown on national television. Local TV news personages would visit for interviews at our various worksites, which included community housing built for members of the Gypsy (Roma) community and several primary schools, as well as work on the newly created

Peace Garden at the Orphan Village.

Our work with orphans proved to be a powerful way for us to rediscover the simple essence of our responsibilities as members of one universal family.

"The Orphan Village was started shortly after a deadly uprising in 1956 when the Communist Party ruled the country with the support of the Soviet Union. The Hungarian people at that time took to the streets in hopes of finding greater freedom, but, before long, those hopes were crushed by Soviet tanks. The fighting turned many children into orphans and left many without a home.

"The Orphan Village was a humanitarian response to the need of that time. In its peak years, the village hosted over 200 young girls and boys. When our team arrived, the

orphanage was guided by a visionary man who believed that the children needed to have more than their basic external needs satisfied. He envisioned them having a 'sacred space', an environmentally beautiful area, a setting where children could come to pray or just sit quietly and reflect.

"Our volunteers happily took on the challenge and helped shape a Peace Garden, aided by local donations of dozens of species of bamboo trees and a wide variety of flowers and greenery. The garden and pond belonged to all the children and staff. They were free to use the beauty there to find peace and renewal.

"There was rich satisfaction in landscaping, planting, and shaping the picturesque Peace Garden, and this was multiplied by the willingness of so many children to join in and help. As the project moved forward, you could see Hungarian orphans on the shoulders of Uncle Kerim from Ghana and others holding hands with Auntie Fazida from Singapore or playing soccer with Uncle Sergio from Spain. The orphans were no longer isolated; their faces expressed their joy at finding that the world had now provided them with many caring uncles and aunts. These experiences were living proof to each of us that we are part of a global family.

"Poet Maya Angelou offered this insight: 'I've learned that people will forget what you said, people will forget what you did, but people will never forget what you made them feel.' The orphans made us feel deeply appreciated, and we made them feel they had family members after all, even if their parents were no longer on earth.

"At RYS, we believed that loving acts of service were visible examples of God's spirit being visited on a community. Many participants were gifted with a rich faith. While faith is an important gift, it needs to be wed to love for it to fulfill its full potential. Love grows in the fertile soil of service. When those gifted with faith exercise it through selfless service, a path is illuminated for those struggling to come out of the darkness.

"This was illustrated when the RYS met Nora, Hanna, and Zoe, who had grown up in the industrial city of Pecs in southwest Hungary. Just twenty years old, they were searching to discover interesting people and have fun. While working to repair housing for local gypsy families, our team members noticed the three stopping to observe us. We wondered if it was our diversity, our interactions, or simply the happiness we felt doing our work that caught their curiosity. Later, Hanna would explain that their imagination was captured by what seemed to be the world visiting their community.

"In time, Hanna and the girls began approaching our volunteers and striking up conversations. The Hungarian girls learned that our group had come from many nations and that each volunteer came with a unique religious background. Hanna was surprised about how well we harmonized. She quizzed us, asking, 'Aren't you supposed to be enemies?' It was clear that we broke her concepts as we laughed and joked while working together. Coming from different religions was not going to keep us from enjoying each other or from our work.

"These three friends considered themselves agnostics; they did not believe in God, but they did not close their minds to the possibility. This exposure to religious people was a new experience because they had grown up in an environment where religious freedom and cultural exchange were limited. The schools they had attended promoted atheism as a more scientific approach to life and often put down religion as a form of superstition.

"Soon, Hanna asked if the three could join our work team. As we all shared a desire to help the local gypsy families, the decision was easy.

"Hanna shared with us one evening about herself and her friends. She said, 'We were not interested in religion when we were growing up. It did not mean anything to us. We were not against those people who believed, but we were not inspired by them either. When things started to change, with the new freedoms, those church groups just focused on taking care of themselves; they did not really try to help those outside the group.

'Your group is so different; it is like a universal family. You have people coming from each country and religion, and they are all reaching out to help people that need help. You are doing something particularly good, and yet you will go back home not asking anything from us. This is a hugely different spirit than anything we have experienced. This unbelievable attitude makes us want to know why you are doing this. We want to know what it is that inspires you. Is it God?'

"Was it God?" The Grandfather asked them, his eyes sparkling. "Well, it is my feeling that how we act, care for, and love those in our midst carries much greater importance than our religious labels.

"To Hanna, God seemed to be seen in the hearts, words, and hands of those offering loving service. They belonged to Christians, Muslims, Buddhists, and Hindus, all serving to add a unique expression of that love.

"These words are a reminder of what many young people are expecting from religion. Religion needs to be relevant; it needs to be driven by a desire to improve the lives of humanity.

"I am sure some of you are religious. We people of faith are meant to be harbingers of the fullness of life. What matters is that our words and deeds help to connect others to the loving Source of our global family by taking care of our brothers and sisters who are in need. That, to me, is what true religion is all about: loving others."

The Grandfather noticed a frown on Kyle's face.

"Kyle?" He asked with concern. "Is there something worrying you?"

"So, can atheists and agnostics do service projects and love others?"

The Grandfather laughed. "Of course! Hannah and her friends became the first agnostics on the Religious Youth Service! It didn't bother them, and it didn't bother us. Like us, they were people of goodwill. When men and women of goodwill work together for a noble purpose, the world will come to understand and realize the greatest hopes and dreams of humanity. Anyone can love; anyone can serve."

Juan thought he detected looks of relief on some students' faces. They seemed glad to know that they did not have to be religious or from a particular religion to help others in the world.

He was relieved too, but for a different reason. The happy faces of the orphans and their joy in the international project gave him hope. He was not an orphan; he still had his mother. Yet the story seemed to him a promise that one day he would be happy again, even after the loss of his father.

Chapter 11: Coffee Pots of Hope

"The future belongs to those who give the next generation

reason for hope."

Pierre Teilhard de Chardin

"Whoa!" said Kyle. "What's with the little cups?"

"They're called demitasse cups," said Chrissy, elbowing him. "Don't be so rude."

The Grandfather, with several students' help, was passing out what appeared to be mini coffee cups. The cups were followed up with a shot of richly dark coffee in each.

"You might want to use a little more sugar than you are used to," said the Grandfather. "This is extremely strong coffee. Some call it dark lightning. If any of you have to stay up studying tonight for an exam, you're in luck! This is powerful, Turkish coffee, the type you pour into little cups because big cups would be way too much caffeine. Drink too much of this strong but tasty coffee, and you might start to speak rapidly or, possibly, have to rush to a toilet."

He could see the students appreciating the strong smell of the coffee. Then some delicately sipped at the demitasse cups.

"Good, good," he said. "Take it slowly. Don't drink it all at once. If you have a second cup, you might find your hair standing on end."

The students laughed. Some of the male students drained their cups and wanted the challenge of a second

one.

"No, no," Mr. Bennet protested. "I don't want your parents calling me and telling me some of you chattered all night after school!"

"Well, my friends," said the Grandfather, "let me tell you about a time I drank 18 cups of that coffee. I don't think I slept well for a couple of days after that, and my stomach was in knots! My teeth were chattering! But I did it for love — and for service.

"You know, there is something almost sacred about people gathering around a hot drink and talking. I'm sure, when you go out for a cup of coffee with your best friend, the object of the outing is not the coffee itself. It's just an excuse to facilitate communication. And so it was with me, with my 18 cups of coffee."

The Grandfather put his cup of coffee on a small stand and began: "Pierre Teilhard de Chardin, a noted philosopher, scientist, and Jesuit priest offered this insightful observation: 'The future belongs to those who give the next generation reason for hope.' I hope the upcoming story can offer you some reason to hope and support you in your efforts to shape a better, kinder future.

"When Eastern Europe and the Soviet Union went through their period of transition, the glue that held Yugoslavia together came apart. Formed by a treaty after World War I, the nation of Yugoslavia had been pasted together across ethnic, religious, and cultural lines. Following the collapse of the Soviet Union, great transformation took place throughout Eastern Europe. Out of what was Yugoslavia, a handful of newly reorganized nations worked to establish their own governments.

"With a history of ethnic conflict, the region was filled with mutual resentment, fear, and distrust that were easily reignited. The emergence of a self-governing Croatia was marked by a time of violent ethnic conflict that broke out into war in the southern parts of the nation.

"European newspapers and television splashed images daily of the violence in the region. A group of RYS members and their friends in Europe felt an urgency to do something that would help alleviate some of the sufferings. In cooperation with the International Relief Friendship Foundation (IRFF) and Forum East (Austria), they gathered resources and formed a team of volunteers. A camp in Varazdin, Croatia, run by the United Nations' Department for Displaced Persons and Refugees, was selected as the work site for an RYS project.

"The RYS project drew its volunteers from 22 countries. Many of the volunteers were college students taking an extended spring break. When they arrived at Camp Varazdin, one of the first things they noticed was that it was filled with the elderly, women, and young children.

"We soon learned that men and older boys were noticeably absent from the camp because they had stayed behind in the war zone to protect their homes and villages. For the people living in the camps, the absence of those they loved created an anxious longing that drained joy and vitality from their daily lives.

"The camp was a world unto itself and, for most, it was a world of broken dreams and painful memories. Multiple families squeezed into rooms that had the ambience of run-down barracks. Privacy existed only in one's thoughts. Material possessions were few and simple, often consisting of what could be carried away on short notice from their previous homes. Memories of death and destruction became even more oppressive due to the gnawing anxiety of not knowing the fate of loved ones or the destiny of their community.

"In contrast to the psyche of camp residents, our volunteers were enthusiastic and full of dreams. Most came from more prosperous and peaceful areas in Europe and the USA and had lived lives free from the daily realities of fear, violence, and economic displacement. Some of the volunteers wondered aloud about their personal ability to do something 'for these people'—something that would really make a difference. Looking at the suffering before their eyes, they half-complained that they lacked the depth or ability to touch it, ease it, or provide anything from their own lives that would be of real help.

"Technically speaking, those living in the camps were called displaced persons and not refugees. Displaced persons are those driven away from their homes to another part of the country, whereas refugees come from other countries. Although the UN did its best to care for those in their charge, the continuous influx of displaced families presented enormous challenges for the under-supplied and understaffed camp.

"One example of the growing needs was in the feeding of the residents. The food that we shared in the dining hall was not enough to satisfy a healthy calorie intake. Part of the lethargy of those at the camp was related to this fact. To supplement the diet, we contributed sacks of special fish powder that our partner organization, the IRFF, had donated.

"We knew that the fish powder was high in protein and that the IRFF had used it in Rwandan refugee camps where it was of great help. We received permission to add the nutritious powder to the large pots of soup and eventually used it in many of the dishes that were prepared. The fish powder proved to be an excellent supplement to the camp's diet. Many residents noted an increase in their energy levels, and some commented that they thought they were starting to put on a little additional weight.

"We were charged with painting the large public dining room and the crowded dorm rooms where the families bunked together. In addition, we decided to fix the shared toilet facilities and transform a small storage room into a nursery. The hearts of the volunteers toward the work were filled with sincerity. Each person was determined to do their best to make things work and look better.

147

"On the morning of the second day at the camp, we joined with the community for meals in the large dining hall. We were a little anxious because we were going to start our work and meet many new people. It was hard not to feel like strangers in a strange land. During the meal, a few of the more outgoing children from the camp ventured up to us to start some form of communication, but soon language differences seemed to end the exchange.

"On the third day at the worksite, the morning sun welcomed us with promise as the air clung to an early morning chill. Teams began scraping and preparing walls and ceilings for painting. After completing a few good hours of work, we neared the time when our teams would take a short break to have a light snack and socialize. It was at this point that a simple, somewhat funny event took place that would change the direction of our relationship with the community.

"Adem and I were part of a work team that was painting the outside of a barracks. A few minutes before our team was called to have a break, we were approached unexpectedly by a woman who looked much older than her age. She faced Adem but inquired in a voice that addressed those in her presence, 'Would you like me to make you some coffee?' Adem and I eagerly nodded our agreement. The woman quietly went off to prepare.

"British-born, Adem was of Turkish descent, and his facial appearance was much like that of many of the ethnic Bosnians living in the camp. The woman who was making coffee for us took an immediate liking to Adem, for he looked somewhat like her own son and was of a similar age.

"Bosnia bordered Croatia, and ethnic populations mixed and overlapped freely throughout much of history. Much of the area had been under Turkish Ottoman rule for hundreds of years, and there was much intermarriage. One result of this historical legacy was that children of Bosnians often had a strong resemblance to their Turkish neighbors.

"Adem and I continued to work as we waited for the coffee to arrive. A shout from a staff member arose, announcing that our 'official' time for a work-break snack had begun. The rest of the team was growing impatient and decided to leave the worksite to go to the area where the staff had prepared food and beverages.

"As time passed, Adem and I began to doubt if the coffee was really going to appear. Maybe we did not understand what the lady was saying? Maybe we should leave and join the rest of the teams and have our snack?

"After a considerable length of time, the woman appeared with her pot of Turkish coffee—strong Turkish coffee. Adem and I stared at the pot and the cups and, after some hesitation, quietly decided to accept the lady's offering of hospitality. We were partners in the challenge to drain the pot of coffee that was prepared for the whole team. As we poured and drank and poured and drank, the woman was pleased and began to share her story:

"'My husband and two sons are at the front where the fighting is happening. I have not heard from them in over a year. It is so hard to get news from the front. I do not know if they are dead or alive. I hope they are alive; I feel they are alive, but I do not know. I do believe they are alive.'

"She was pouring out more of her story with each cup of coffee that we drank. At the point when we began to think we were close to the end of the pot, another woman appeared with another full pot of coffee. She also was expecting the team but disappointedly found only Adem and me.

"Adem and I knew without speaking what we should do. By drinking the coffee, we were showing our appreciation and covering for our missing teammates. These women had so little. They were offering what they could, sharing the best thing they had with us.

"So we drank and drank and mostly listened while these two women shared their stories. When the pots were nearly bone-dry, the count was 18 cups for me, 22 cups for Adem. We would pay the price for this, but the reward of having these women share their stories was well worth it.

"The next day, the woman again appeared and offered coffee. This time we made sure that it was going to be shared by the whole team. The women continued to share with us as if we were their long-lost relatives. On our last day at the camp, the women from the barracks prepared cake from their meager rations to go along with the now-traditional coffee ceremony.

"As the women in the camp gathered, they began to share through a translator:

"'Sometimes people came to our camp and left things at our door. Sometimes we can use those things, sometimes not. It was clear they did not really care what we needed, for they never asked. Your group came to the camps and worked, shared, and ate the same food as us. You listened to us, you played with the children, and you tried to help as best as you could. What I want to say to you is that, when you were here, we realized that we were not forgotten. Because of you, we had some time where we could put aside the war and just share life. Thank you for giving us hope.'

"The words of these women gave us insight into the deeper reasons for our coming to the camp in Varazdin. These women appreciated our fixing and repairing the living situation of the camp, but that could have been accomplished by professional workers. What the mothers really needed to know was that people still cared for them and wanted to be of help. Our open-hearted service was personal confirmation that they were not forgotten and that they were indeed valued. This was a gift that money could not buy.

"The insecurities of the volunteers disappeared as we realized we had much more to give than we expected. Through the heart of service, we experienced the liberating power of giving hope. The volunteers understood more clearly that their lives were not simply for themselves but that they lived to help and encourage others.

"The women of Varazdin helped open my eyes and bring me to an important realization. While fixing buildings for those in need is a virtuous activity, it is not an essential part of our work. The most critical element of our work is to help heal the human heart and to uplift and celebrate the human spirit. The women, in offering us coffee from their meager supply, made a beautiful, selfless offering. By accepting the coffee and listening to their stories, we were accepting and recognizing their hearts. They felt this and, in turn, were able to accept and appreciate the efforts we were making.

"One year after our time in Varazdin, the fighting in the southern part of Croatia concluded. Most of those living in the camps returned to their villages and our hopes and prayers were always that all the women would have a grand reunion with their husbands and sons. Those in the camps profoundly deserved a chance to rediscover joy."

The Grandfather noticed that, as Chrissy, Juan, Kyle, and others collected the cups and saucers, some of the students offered them up with both hands, as if they were handling something precious — even holy.

Chapter 12: Down with the Gun and Up with the Hoe

"The power of one if fearless and focused, is formidable, but the power of many working together is better"
Gloria Macapagal Arroyo, former president of the
Philippines

Mr. Bennet led the class up the slight rise that led to the Grandfather's house. Everyone knew that Juan, Chrissy, Kyle, and a couple of others had been sent ahead to prepare something special. All were looking forward to seeing what it was. This was way better than being in class all the time!

As they approached, they heard the faint sound of drums, both with the rattle of drumsticks and the thump of the heels of hands. Then they heard singing, but not the song as they knew it. This was almost like an exuberant chant, punctuated by the rattling and pounding of the drums. As they drew nearer, their ears told them that the chants were not in English.

Coming into sight of the Grandfather's gate, they saw Chrissy dressed in a colorful skirt and blouse with a furry animal skin tied around her waist. She was shaking the animal skin and making swan-like gestures with her hands. Juan and Kyle were wearing dashiki shirts and pounding away at skin-headed drums, Kyle wildly palming his drums and Juan splaying drumsticks. There were neighbors lined up too, colorfully dressed and participating in the exuberant chant.

Flattered by the welcoming committee, the students rather shyly filed past them to go up to the Grandfather, who was standing in the doorway of his home, also dressed in a colorful dashiki, his arms wide as if in a communal hug for them all.

"Welcome!" he shouted exuberantly. "Welcome to Africa!"

Laughing and with pleased smiles on their faces, the students followed his direction into the backyard and garden area. The "African" troubadours followed them, drumming behind them as if to herd them there, exuberantly continuing the song and rhythms. Some of the students began to clap and dance along.

The students were still chuckling as the Grandfather explained that he was serenaded similarly with the most beautiful welcome music in a village in Uganda in all his travels. He described how the local villagers had lined the road and sang to welcome the international volunteers as they walked toward the school where they would soon begin work.

The Grandfather shared how the rhythm of the drums took over, and as observers, they found their bodies irresistibly moving. With a longing in his voice, he expounded on how the drumming in this village was unmatched. Only in the South Pacific island of Tonga had he found comparable vocal harmonies too.

The Grandfather led his audience in applause for the performers.

"With very little notice," he said, "they managed to capture the sounds and much of the spirit of Africa, and they have brought it here to my backyard. Juan, here, seems to have a special ability to make good and exciting things happen. I would love to find out what special ability each of you has, for that is part of your gift to the world."

Juan took the words in and made a slight nod of acknowledgement, but he kept his head ducked, finding the recognition from the elder a little embarrassing.

The smells of the African foods the neighbors had prepared met their nostrils. There were matoke, cassava, and sweet potatoes — some of the favorite foods of Ugandans.

"Unfortunately, the great spirit and culture of Africa have too often been torn by civil war," the Grandfather began. "So while we begin joyously, and while we believe in the lively spirit of African people, we must acknowledge the reality of war on that fabulous continent as well. For Africa is fabulous, yes. It has great people, and its physical beauty and the variety of its animals and other life forms are overwhelming.

"Yet despite its beauty, living in Lira, Uganda in the year 2000 offered many challenges to the average citizen. Most families in Lira District made their living from the soil, and the margin of error separating them from impoverishment was often as narrow as a prolonged drought. Parents struggled to find ways to pay for their children's school uniforms, books, and modest school fees. For most, receiving an elementary school education was the last opportunity to receive formal classroom schooling.

"Attitudes among school children in Lira differed from what I was used to seeing. Children uncomplainingly walked long distances to school in uniforms that they wore

Courtesy of Stephen Hall Photography

with obvious pride. The school day was a learning opportunity and a way to a brighter future. In Lira, the conformity in dress was easily accepted, as school was understood to be for learning, not for fashion statements.

"Educational institutes in Lira and throughout Uganda were largely started by religious organizations, and many have remained in their care. One can learn a lot about people by observing how they care for things. If you were to visit a typical classroom, you would see in its simplicity, cleanliness, and care that spoke much to the cultural ethos of the community.

"While visiting the same school, you would likely observe students gathered in small, segregated clusters, boys on one side and girls on the other. Watching the activities and interaction between students and instructors, an observer can recognize a fine balance of spontaneity and protocols. Respectfulness is a word that describes the environment well.

"Prior to our RYS team's arrival, there was considerable unrest spilling into the Lira District that in part was agitated by warlords from neighboring Sudan. Gun-toting recruiting agents representing the warlords targeted areas where poverty sank its teeth bone-deep. For some frustrated fathers, a political enemy appeared as an easier opponent than that of remorseless poverty. Some good people were torn between the choice of picking up guns in hopes of shaping a better future or ignoring the cries of their hungry children. It was not a situation that can easily be judged on a full stomach.

"Lira had been the site of gunfights and killing between rebels and police. Fortunately, many of the raiding combatants lacked a deep emotional commitment to their fight. It was during a lull in the violence that my friend Massimo Trombin came to Lira as part of his work as European Director of the International Relief Friendship Foundation (IRFF). In researching ways for the IRFF to serve the community better, Massimo met a young rebel leader. I'll call him Michael.

"After an initial 'feeling out period', Michael shared with Massimo his background and offered his own thoughts and experiences involving the rural poor. As trust deepened, Michael shared the reasons why he originally decided to pick up arms and what was needed to have him put down his gun. It might have been because they shared the same birthday, but clearly, something aligned in their relationship. Soon Michael and Massimo became good friends. The two were destined to work together on projects that would help local civilians and reach those that wanted to turn in their guns and rejoin society.

"In listening and sharing with Michael and others, Massimo realized that by having more attractive economic alternatives, families would not be easily swayed by the offers or the threats of the rebels. Massimo began thinking and shaping a plan to provide families a path towards greater economic security. Turning to his network of friends, Massimo sought advice from Mr. Rutangye, a native Ugandan who was an environmental education leader in the national government.

"Mr. Rutangye was consistently putting together practical and sustainable projects for the benefit of Ugandan farmers. Rutangye suggested that his work with a new high-grade banana plant in another region could work well in the Lira District. This new banana plant would

Courtesy Wikimedia Commons

allow each tree to produce more fruit, and more fruit meant more profit for the local farmer.

"While improving the yield on bananas was an important benefit for local farmers, Rutangye also wanted to pioneer the growth of a cash crop new to the area: coffee. Timing is critical in the field of agriculture, and the timing seemed favorable to Lira farmers. A spike in the worldwide coffee market was making it economical to open new areas for coffee cultivation. The Lira district had rich soil and a suitable climate to produce a fine grade of coffee. For families in Lira, a good coffee crop could open educational doors for more children and help them break free of the gravity of poverty.

"Massimo and Mr. Rutangye worked on a plan to help make that happen. As the plan developed, the International RYS Director, myself, was called in to have RYS international volunteers contribute their piece to that plan.

"Our combined team worked with an understanding that successful development projects should be designed to be as sustainable as possible. Poor families predictably suffer from a lack of capital, so it is better to draw on local knowledge and skills whenever possible. Why should villagers spend precious money on buying something from another area if they can find an adequate local replacement? Why import expensive experts to fix things when you can make it work using local materials and local expertise?

"Indigenous knowledge and insights can differ from town to town, region to region, nation to nation. An example of how this knowledge can be used occurred in work in Lira. In Lira, harmful fungi grow on the unprotected roots of banana plants and hinder or kill their growth. Instead of purchasing a high-priced chemical spray manufactured in a distant country, Mr. Rutangye brought a solution he learned in another part of Uganda. He showed local trainees that dipping the roots of the banana cuttings into a diluted mixture of water and cow urine prevented the fungi from growing. Cow urine is free, readily available, and not harmful to the soil, so a local solution to a problem was found in sharing indigenous knowledge.

"The process of effectively linking new ideas and methods to indigenous knowledge requires local community involvement. The help of a well-respected local leader was needed for the Lira community outreach, and that naturally brought us to Betty Okwea, a parliament member. I will tell you more about Mama Betty sometime. She was highly influential, and she loved the plan. She went into action by mobilizing local village councils. The village councils each sent a team of youth leaders to join our project, as they considered local agricultural training an essential service. After completing the training, Mr. Rutangye and his staff provided the seeds and plantings for the graduates to take back to their villages.

"The graduates of the program were charged with teaching farmers the 'new' methods and passing on the seedlings to those in their villages. The initial training program had a ripple effect as villages picked up on what was learned. The efforts spread, and they helped reshape the way agriculture was done in the district. With the tools and knowledge provided, each youth leader brought home an opportunity for his area's farms to more than double their annual income.

"In Lira, as in other communities suffering from violent civil strife, people long for the day when the guns are put down. Rebels who take the huge step of turning in their guns are called Returnees. For the Returnee, it is an exceedingly difficult transition to go from an outlaw soldier to civilian life. Often, the stinging poverty and troubles that they fled await them on their return. Michael, while transitioning from rebel leader to Returnee, regularly discussed with Massimo the challenges that came when a person chose to put away his gun and return home.

"The agricultural work that Massimo helped to introduce to village leaders caught Michael's attention, as it offered the promise of improving his situation. Michael also realized that the potential increase in agricultural yields could lure many other rebels away from guns.

"Resentment towards the rebels was real in Lira, and a process was needed to help make it easier for all parties to reconcile and live together. Massimo decided to give IRFF support to an agricultural project aimed to serve the widows of rebels, as they often were in very desperate situations. To the citizens of Lira, the widows were much easier to sympathize with than that did the actual fighting. After the success of this program with widows, the IRFF opened participation to actual Returnees. Rebels began to turn in their guns and pick up their hoes.

"The program's success helped nearly two hundred men make the transition and return to their families. In a short time, the larger community began to recognize the value of these efforts, and they encouraged Minister Betty Okwea to report the success to the national government. Leaders in the government saw the project as a model for encouraging Returnees, and they began to adopt it in different parts of Uganda.

Courtesy BBC

"It is true that all the world's rebels are not that way because of poverty. Yet, as members of humanity, we can and should work to offer people in desperate situations an acceptable alternative to violence. If one answer to the sting of poverty was found in something as mundane as cow urine, a hybrid banana seedling, and a coffee bean, how many other answers are waiting to be discovered and implemented? When given an acceptable choice, people choose life and peace.

"It is important to look at issues from a variety of viewpoints in coming up with acceptable solutions. To find a lasting solution to civil strife, a problem solver needs to understand both the rebels and the heart and motivation of those who refused to pick up a weapon. The Returnees had abandoned their close-knit community and the social norms that guided it. For those that stayed home, it was not easy to simply embrace those who had inflicted additional suffering on their families.

"Returnees were justifiably afraid of retribution. Massimo realized this problem and offered a solution based on the concept of restorative justice. Only a year before, rebels were periodically raiding in Lira, and in one case, they killed a local police officer. Returnees needed to do more than saying they were sorry for their past; they had to pay some price for their wrongdoings. Yet, that price had to be one that would not add to the burden of resentment, violence, and hatred.

"Massimo had an ingenious plan that he proposed to Michael. 'Since your group killed a policeman who was just doing his job, you will need to do something for the police. Why don't you build an extension to the overcrowded police station? They really need one. This is a way you can show the police and the community that you really are sorry, and it is a clear demonstration that you want to be a part of society again.'

"Healing broken hearts is a key to healing a broken world. When we reconcile with our former enemies and shed tears and sweat for their sake, we will create a healing force that will help us avoid bloodshed. We will be true peacemakers.

"Massimo really did have the right idea. Yet beyond the idea, he was a person who spent his life living out the ideals that feed the hope of peace. In a sense, his dynamic and creative energy was the substance of peace in action.

"Never, please never forget, the power of one person to do a lot of good in this world. Massimo's efforts helped change a village, and those changes helped inspire changes throughout a country. In changing one man through friendship, he brought a wave of peace to those who were at war with one another.

"I am reminded of the words of the Philippines former President, Gloria Macapagal Arroyo, 'The power of one if fearless and focused, is formidable, but the power of many working together is better.'

"Please, never say, 'I'm only just one person. What can I do?' Next week, my friends, I will talk about the power of one person and how that power can inspire many. The keys to world peace and prosperity are in every individual human heart— especially when that heart

169

inspires the hearts of others to pitch in and work for goodness. Thank you.

"Now, Juan, Chrissy, Kyle—let's have some more of that African music!"

Chapter 13: The Heart of Wanting To Be Together

"The deepest level of communication is not communication, but communion. It is wordless . . . beyond speech . . beyond concept."

Thomas Merton

Music of the mysterious, sibilant sitar filled the room as people entered the home and met with the greeting of the Grandfather. No one said anything. Music master Ravi Shankar was able to cast a spell over an audience even through recorded music. With silent gestures, Juan, Chrissy, Kyle, and the Grandfather directed the students to take seats. Then they quietly passed out a variety of Indian teas in cups.

As some of the students began to breathe deeply and lower their eyelids, the Grandfather smiled. The magic of music was working on them, conveying peace, beauty, and a longing satisfied by the assurance of the loveliness of the instrumentation. It carried with it India's long history of spirituality and the sanctity of daily life.

As the music continued, the Grandfather noted a few tears were seeping from under Chrissy's lowered eyelashes. Other students raised their heads, their faces serene in a kind of gratitude. One student put her hand on her heart.

"It seems to be playing on my spine," said one student suddenly. "Like a massage of little gold bubbles!"

"I can feel it in my heels," said another, her face breaking out in a satisfied smile. "Tingling. Giving me wings on my feet."

Everyone else continued the silence. Everyone was breathing deeply in a kind of spontaneous meditation. When the strains of the string became particularly poignant, students tilted their heads, feeling the music. Some mouths were open in awe. Micro expressions of pain creased the young people's eyes as the music spoke of human suffering. It ended on shimmering strings kiting upward in the promise of spiritual love.

There was silence. The Grandfather let it sink in.

"What kind of instrument was that?" asked Juan.

"A sitar. It looks something like a long-necked ukulele."

Mr. Bennet said, "I've never heard anything so relaxing."

Many heads turned to him to say things like, "I know, right?" "I feel like all my joints and muscles just loosened up", and "I'm going to melt into a puddle on the floor!"

"Don't do that," chuckled Mr. Bennet. "We'll have to put you back together again to walk back to school."

The Grandfather smiled.

"What sort of things do you associate with India?" he asked the class.

The students looked thoughtful.

"Elephants."

"Sacred cows."

"The River Ganges."

"The Taj Mahal."

"Millions and billions of people — all wearing white."

"Heat!"

"Yes," the Grandfather said. "India is all that, and temple bells and mountains. It is a vast and beautiful land. It is a nation, but it is also a subcontinent and, in some ways, a world of its own. Within the arms of her boundaries are over one billion souls. India's people are members of all the world's religions, and they speak a score of languages. It is the home of brilliant genius and entrepreneurship as well as the world's largest illiterate population, with millions living in abject poverty. Warm hearts and cold indifference sleep in the same city, separate yet together.

"Mohandas K. Gandhi and his philosophy of nonviolence helped stimulate the gigantic nation's march forward on its path to political independence from Great Britain in 1948. Gandhi's deep spiritual gift was rooted in his ability to embody the high principles that he taught. His personal character, coupled with his practice of non-violent resistance, provided a base for a peaceful transition from colonial rule to national independence.

"When the quest for independence was nearly achieved, less noble ambitions began to emerge and pull apart dreams of a peaceful transition. Against Gandhi's wishes, the independence movement divided along religious lines, with notable Muslim leaders demanding and receiving a separate state. Partitioning India and creating Pakistan as a separate Muslim state created instability that led millions to migrate from their traditional homes. The trek of the displaced often went through hostile terrain and led the sojourners to destinations that were unfamiliar and ill-prepared to receive them.

"Anxiety, fear, and violence grew in anticipation of and following the midnight partition of India. Questions concerning the fate of neighbors, family, and friends were at the forefront of people's hearts and minds. Would those departing arrive in their new communities safely? Who would take over abandoned homes and property? How were the people going to survive in their new 'homes'?

"Tensions mounted as news coverage reported deadly attacks initiated by religious militants and bandits. Human caravans of migrant families—Hindu, Muslim, and Sikh, passed through unpoliced lands on the journey to find new homes. Many did not make it. Often, violence begot violence.

"Fissures between religions are often aggravated by selfish human behavior. The carnage that marked the birth of Pakistan as a Muslim state and India as a secular nation was the antithesis of Gandhi's dream. India and Pakistan were like resentful siblings—brothers who were jealous of and came to hate one another. "Throughout its long history, India has served as the home of much of humanity's rich spiritual heritage. Various spiritual currents identified as a part of contemporary Hinduism have flowed into her basin for nearly three millennia. One result of this extensive historic process is that Hinduism embraces multiple expressions of truth in the pursuit of human liberation. The holy men of Hinduism, the Sufi masters of Islam, and the founding gurus of Sikhism all grasped the simple eternal wisdom that truth is found from many sources.

"Traditionally, the heart of India has been her villages. Amicable relationships between co-religionists living in tens of thousands of villages spread across the subcontinent provided an essential element for the stability of society. At times, this stability is threatened, and with it, the delicate balance of daily life collapses.

In recent decades, political interests have manipulated religious sentiments. At times, they have agitated for courses of action that have led to violence and a loss of innocent lives. Today, a tense and threatening relationship exists between contemporary India and Pakistan as they face each other, armed with conventional and nuclear weapons. Decades of reciprocal antipathy between the neighboring states have resulted in a costly drain of capital, energy, and creativity.

"Under the right conditions, India and Pakistan, born from the same 'mother', share the ability to reconcile and develop a new and mutually beneficial relationship. Yet even if a contemporary leader of the moral stature of 'Mahatma' Gandhi would emerge, he or she would need the support of 'coalitions of the caring'—coalitions of people with the willingness and insight to work across religious and national boundaries and having the capacity to mobilize people and resources essential in reshaping the region's economy.

"Establishing mutually beneficial cooperation between people and nation-states is an essential factor needed to wrest millions from the grip of illiteracy and poverty. Decisive to achieve such an outcome is establishing a perspective and level of unity that transcends any singular religious identity. In both the nations of India and Pakistan, there are forces working for and against such a reconciliation. Whoever wins the hearts of the youth will maintain the advantage in deciding the outcome.

"The city of Ayodhya holds claim to having been founded nearly 9,000 years ago. Known as the City of Worship, it is one of the seven sacred cities of India. The city is considered to be the birthplace of Lord Ram, a major personage in the Hindu pantheon. In ancient times, the Ram Janmabhoon Temple was built at the site of the birthplace of Lord Ram, but in 1528 during the Moghul era, the Muslim leader constructed the Babri Mosque over the ruins of the temple. The mosque for Muslims was a site of worship, but to some Hindus, it was a painful reminder of something taken away from their heritage.

"In December 1992, outside the Babri Mosque, a crowd of 150,000 Hindu demonstrators gathered in the daytime to protest. The protesters were demanding to reclaim the grounds as sacred to Hindus and to remove the offending mosque. In the dark of night, a large group returned to 'reclaim their heritage' and tore down the old mosque, declaring that it would be replaced by something suitable for Hindus.

"Unfortunately, the destruction of the Barbri Mosque occurred during a dangerous confluence of political and religious influences. Within Islam, a radicalized political segment was emerging. Adherents called on 'Believers' to reclaim all lands formerly under Muslim rule, and this included much of India.

"Concurrently, the Hindu-centered ideology of Hindutva was gaining political influence among Indians, and its adherents sought to make India exclusively a Hindu country or at least grant Hindus privileged status. Mutual fear and mistrust between Hindu and Muslims were growing to dangerous levels. Extremism was becoming more pronounced.

"With the news of the Barbri Mosque's destruction, a series of bloody riots ignited across India. Beyond the border, in Bangladesh and Pakistan, which are nations with large Muslim populations, rioters were reported to have burned down 17 Hindu temples. Each side had grievances, but those grievances were too often taken out into the streets. The deep spirituality that lay at the heart of both religions was being pushed aside, and violence and hatred were filling the vacuum.

"During this dynamic time, I was in India representing RYS and preparing a series of events in multiple cities aimed at promoting interreligious harmony. Following the destruction of the Barbri Mosque, the riots and spontaneous violence in Bombay (Mumbai) created a situation where people felt it was too dangerous to make unnecessary travel. We experienced this firsthand when our taxi driver refused to drive in certain areas. Even in the places where he felt safe, the tension was palpable. While in Bombay, we decided that it was best to cancel our main program.

"Our experience with the RYS interfaith program the next day in New Delhi proved a vastly different experience. The behavior of those who braved the violence and troubles in the capital and ventured to the seminar re-opened my eyes to the valuable impact that interreligious programs can have on attitudes and actions.

"In the role of International RYS Director, I often set up training programs for college-age students and working youth. These programs were aimed at preparing potential participants with the communication and cross-cultural skills necessary for participation and leadership in international service. The New Delhi program was fortunate to attract compassionate youth who religiously identified as Hindu, Sikh, Roman Catholic, Muslim, Jain, Parsi, Christian, and Unificationist.

"While violence and threats were taking place in the New Delhi streets, those participants attending the seminar made the decision to seek understanding, compassion, and cooperation as the appropriate response to fear and resentment. As my experiences in India have many times reminded me, it is often the young, spiritually-minded believer who can best grasp that all are valued members of one human family. That commonality is beyond any specific religious identity since it points to a Transcendent

Source, a source we are all connected to.

"During our meetings in New Delhi, we worked in small groups and shared with each other issues close to our hearts. So many of the conversations revolved around how we could become better equipped to help improve the lives of others. Each day, the media covered the news of violence throughout the nation but, unknown to the public, these young adults and others like them had chosen a special path: the path of service to all of humanity.

"A crisis can trigger substantial personal reflection. Our meeting during a time of social turbulence provided an atmosphere where each participant could more seriously examine their own lives. While the energy generated in small group discussions was at times vibrant, it was complemented by periods of quiet reflection and deep sharing.

"We shared stories of our heroes and the virtues they displayed, virtues that allowed them to stand out in the crowd. We examined our own strengths and weaknesses and noted areas where we wanted to develop to become more 'heroic'. The more we talked, the more we saw lines of connection—in our hopes, in the things we admired, in what we valued.

"As our trust grew, we shared with each other the things that were holding us back from being the people we were meant to be. We allowed ourselves to speak about unspoken hopes and dreams as if we were among intimate family members. With hearts full, participants found freedom to express themselves in ways beyond conventional social structures.

"Time passed so quickly that, when it was announced that our meeting time had passed, it took us by surprise. Participants were warned that we should not linger because of the increased potential of the danger facing those traveling.

"The announcement met with some strong resistance. The participants were extremely comfortable with each other and showed no desire to leave.

"After some time had passed, I asked some of the participants, 'Why aren't you going home? Things are dangerous out there, and it is getting dark.'

One lady with long dark hair and large eyes looked at me with a facial expression that spoke before her words.

'We are so happy to be sharing; we have so much to share, and we never really get to mix together. The crazy things happening outside are not what we are about. We enjoy being together. We feel like we have discovered missing family members, so it is so hard to let go!'

"This said it all. It was the core of what they were all about. They wanted to build real friendships, and they were not going to be held back by the walls that others had built. They were determined to share with all the members of their family, which included Muslim, Hindu, Sikh, and people of different backgrounds. In my eyes, this desire represented the real hope of India and the hope for establishing lasting peace."

The talk was over, and the tea had been drunk. The Grandfather looked at Mr. Bennet in surprise. Although the students weren't usually terribly anxious to leave, it was clear that today, they wanted to linger. Quiet conversations and sharing went on for about fifteen minutes. Then, slowly, Mr. Bennet raised his hand.

"It's wonderful that you want to be together," he said, "and I hate to interrupt. We have to go back to school now, but I encourage you to continue your conversations on the way there."

Grandfather, observing the students, was pleased. The sights and feelings he was witnessing were a reminder of the words of Thomas Merton: "The deepest level of communication is not communication, but communion. It is wordless . . . beyond speech . . . beyond concept." The Grandfather's smile grew at the awareness of the communion that was being formed and the joy of being a part of it.

For the first time, several girls came up to the Grandfather and hugged him goodbye in a natural, easy way. His eyebrows showed his surprise, but he received their tributes gratefully and gracefully. Some of the boys came up and shook hands.

Juan and Chrissy were the last to go. The Grandfather couldn't hold himself back any longer before these two special students. He couldn't speak as the pair lay their hands on his shoulders and patted him comfortingly. Several tears fell into his lap.

With the silent wisdom of the sitar music, neither of them spoke or expected the Grandfather to speak. Chrissy's hug and the bow of Juan's head said it all.

As the door was almost closed behind them, the words ripped out of the Grandfather's mouth: "You are so precious to me!"

"And you to us," said Chrissy, clicking the door closed behind her as softly as a kiss.

Chapter 14: Healing the Heart of History

"History, despite its wrenching pain, cannot be unlived, but if faced with courage, need not be lived again."

Maya Angelou

Nobody knew how the fight broke out. Hernando and Joseph had never gotten along, that was for sure. Blue-eyed, fair-skinned Joseph had always had an attitude of superiority to brown-eyed, black-haired Hernando with his olive skin. Hernando spoke accented, casual English, whereas Joseph expressed himself in a patrician way, with perfect enunciation.

As the class was preparing to head out to the Grandfather's, one of Joseph's books splatted on the floor. Hernando, his backpack swinging in the aisle, looked at the book and then to Joseph almost sneeringly. He seemed glad that any trouble had come to Joseph.

"You knocked my book off!" Joseph accused him. "Pick it up!"

"I didn't knock it off," snarled Hernando. "Pick it up yourself!"

"If he did, it was an accident," said Chrissy. "Here. I'll pick it up."

She bent down and picked up the book and handed it to Joseph.

"The spine's broken!" he yelled. "Now I'll have to pay for it! No, Hernando, you'll have to pay for it."

"Boys!" Mr. Bennet brushed past students to get between the two boys, but he was too late. Hernando shoved Joseph with enough force to crush him into a desk, which screeched against the floor. Joseph then got behind the desk and shoved it into Hernando's legs, making him shout out. A girl screamed.

Mr. Bennet managed to get between the two boys. Juan, Kyle, and several other boys pinioned their arms so they couldn't lunge at each other anymore.

"He started it!" yelled Hernando, pulling against his restrainers.

"No, you started it!" screamed Joseph, trying to break free from those holding him.

Mr. Bennet was on his cell phone.

"He's calling security, you guys," warned Chrissy.

The boys calmed down quickly. The security guard was a mean dude. No one wanted anything to do with him.

To their surprise, Mr. Bennet had dialled the Grandfather.

"I'm afraid some of the people in my class are not ready to be people of service," he explained into the cell phone. "They seem to think that violence is still the way to solve problems." Then Mr. Bennet explained what had happened, fairly and factually, so that both Joseph and Hernando nodded as if they felt represented.

Then Mr. Bennet pressed the "Speaker" button, and they all heard the Grandfather's voice floating out of the phone.

"A common reaction to being hurt is to strike back, to avenge a wrong, to even the score," said the Grandfather. "Americans familiar with history know of the bloody feud between two Appalachian families, the Hatfields, and McCoys. After an initial fight, these families chose revenge as a path of redress, a choice that resulted in violence, death, and ruin lasting for generations. Revenge never heals the pain; it just makes it worse in the end. After all, as Gandhi said, 'An eye for an eye only leaves the whole world blind.'

We have the freedom to choose how we respond to injustice. How are you going to respond, boys?"

"The one at fault has to apologize!" Hernando shouted into the phone. Joseph shook his head vehemently in protest.

"Well, Hernando," said the Grandfather. "That certainly makes it easier. What do you do when the other party doesn't think he's wrong, though? Do you just let your anger and resentment eat away at you? And Joseph—are you sure in your accusations that Hernando knocked your book off deliberately? Is it possible he swept it off with his backpack by accident?"

"Hernando has to admit he was wrong," said Joseph adamantly. "Then I'll forgive him."

"There's nothing to forgive!" Hernando all but screamed.

There was a long silence after that. Finally, Hernando spoke into the cell phone.

"I might have accidentally swept his book off his desk with my backpack. If I did, I did not do it deliberately."

"Good, Hernando, good!" cheered the Grandfather. "And Joseph?"

Joseph mumbled, "Well, if it was an accident, okay."

"Accidents do happen," cajoled the Grandfather.

Mr. Bennet sighed. "I'm really duty-bound to report this to the principal. They'll probably both be suspended."

The Grandfather spoke persuasively, "Why don't you let them come along to my home today? You can report them later if you still feel it is important to do so."

Both boys looked pleadingly at Mr. Bennet, and he softened.

"They can come along today," he said. "And I'll base my report—or the lack of it—on their behavior this afternoon," he said, giving each boy a warning glance.

The Grandfather met the solemn group of students at his garden gate when they arrived. He could see everyone was disturbed by the incident.

"It's wet in the garden today," he said. "I'm afraid we'll all have to pack into the living room again. I don't think any neighbors are coming, though. Rain tends to keep people away."

When they were all settled in, the Grandfather asked Joseph and Hernando to come to sit in the front row.

"Such fine, handsome young men," he said. "I hope you will like this story. Sit next to one another. That's right. Hernando, give Joseph a little more elbow room, won't you? Now, thank him, Joseph. A little louder? All right. Let's begin.

"The human heart is the most vulnerable part of our being, yet it is this vulnerability that in large part makes us human. Each human heart has carried within it the pain of sorrow, disappointment, and betrayal while continuously yearning for healing. Personal and historic hurts own a sense of timelessness—they do not simply dissipate. The heart's hurts need treatment, care, sincerity, and patient acts of love to properly heal. Without healing, a hurt can fester and cause irreparable damage to the wounded person.

"The voice of wisdom warns us away from the path of vengeance and points to a less-traveled path. This less-traveled path is difficult, but it can lead to forgiveness, reconciliation, cooperation, and, ultimately, love. The life of Jesus Christ profoundly demonstrates the less-traveled path, and it serves humanity well as a model for healing our hearts.

"I will begin with wise words from Maya Angelou, an eloquent wordsmith: 'History, despite its wrenching pain, cannot be unlived, but if faced with courage, need not be lived again.'

"When we look at history, we can see that both good and evil have been a part of each nation's history. The injustices need to be resolved. The way a nation and its people respond to past injustices can serve either to redress or magnify them. If those hurts are resolved, it opens a path to a deeper level of trust, cooperation, and even shared prosperity.

"All of us living today are inheritors of the fruits of the past, both good and bad. Technology, systems of laws, scientific, and spiritual knowledge are in large part inherited from those who came before us. However, we also have inherited from the past a karmic debt—a debt based on the things that were done with selfish motivation, actions that harmed innocent people. We are constantly seeing the result of these debts. Racial, ethnic, and cultural antagonisms rooted in the past call for reconciliation in the present, or they will remain as a threat to our future well-being.

"For those living in the United States, it is important to realize the long trail of tears that our Native American forerunners have walked. Here, the karmic debt of injustices has yet to be fully paid. Absorbing those tears of sorrow is part of the healing process of this nation. To be a healer of the heart requires a willingness of people to sacrifice for the sake of the aggrieved, i.e., such healing requires sacrificial love.

"Service is the sacrificial love that heals. The path to peace is a rough road that requires personal investment as well as people willing to pioneer pathways for harmonization. For nearly three decades, the RYS has been a catalyst in bringing together young adults from nations, religions, and cultures that have had an adversarial relationship. Turning former enemies into friends is an essential step in generating an environment for lasting peace.

"People tend to come together more substantially when they share a common purpose. Efforts to communicate and work cooperatively can focus on the shared objective. When that objective has universal appeal, such as helping children, needy families, or suffering communities, it becomes especially significant. The RYS places young adults in situations where they are pushed to break through barriers of tradition, racial prejudice, and historic grievances. In working together for a common cause, former antagonisms are oftentimes replaced by warmth of concern and friendship.

"With an awareness of both the historic and current situation of Native Americans, RYS's first director, Mr. Gary Young, decided that the first RYS project in the USA would be to serve the Native American community. The Native American Alcoholic Association (NAAA) in Oakland, California, became the project host, and they invited the RYS to work closely with their staff in a unique endeavor designed to help Native Americans in the San Francisco Bay (Oakland) Area.

"A team of experienced RYS volunteers from 12 nations joined the NAAA staff. This religious and culturally diverse team included Jains, Hindus, Muslims, Sikhs, a young Christian minister from Louisiana, a South African Jew, two Buddhist monks, a female Buddhist scholar from Thailand, and an NGO leader from Nepal.

The youngest participant was Hari Vamsa, a young, blond-haired American girl who was a devotee of Krishna. This amazing mixture of people quickly came together and worked, ate, talked, laughed, shared, and labored side by side with members of the Native American community.

"Many Native Americans face unique dilemmas that are, in part, connected with their often tragic history. Uprooted from their culture and looked down on by large parts of society, individuals often felt adrift, without an anchor. In addition to Alcoholics Anonymous's Twelve Steps, the NAAA approach to healing included finding ways in which participants could positively reconnect to their Native American heritage and experience pride. Low esteem is often a problem with alcoholics, but this problem is magnified for the urban Native American population, who often feel incapable of fitting into the larger culture. The NAAA staff plan had us work on building a traditional Native American sweat lodge to provide medical, spiritual, and psychological support. Sweats are good for the cleansing process in the treatment of alcoholism and various diseases, and a sweat lodge would serve to reconnect the residents to a rich Native American tradition.

"Most of our volunteers were from Asia, having come from Nepal, Thailand, Japan, Korea, and India. They had no direct history of animosity with Native Americans. In a sense, the volunteers were viewed and treated as cousins—part of the community's extended family. Residents quietly found in the relationships with the international volunteers a freedom that arises as trust grows. They were relationships built on purity and mutual concern, and they were relationships that allowed a form of healing to take place.

"Conversations were not the main form of communication; instead, the work was. We, volunteers, put our hearts and sweat into building the lodge. We wanted this lodge to show how much we cared. Our efforts were met by those using the facility with more than equal sincerity, energy, and skill. Young and old found various ways to contribute to each step of the process. As our work neared completion, we gathered around the lodge to offer words of dedication and closing prayer—a deeply emotional experience for everyone present.

"Authentic prayer goes beyond language, flowing beyond the realm of the literal to carry one into a dimension of the imagination. A strong, deep prayer instantly penetrates your heart, liberating you from all that weighs on your soul. A good prayer does not need to be communicated in the language you speak or even in words you understand. Rather, a good prayer, a really blessed prayer, will knock down your barriers and lift you up at the same time.

"There was a Native American elder living at the worksite who was not much of a talker. He joined us whenever he could, and he found various ways to contribute to the ongoing work. We really did not know what he was thinking or feeling about our presence. Soon, however, as in the first eruption of a volcano, we would discover what was hidden beneath his apparently stoic exterior.

"We were closing our work and thought it a good time to form a large circle and share face-to-face with each other about our experiences. The Elder gathered with us in the circle. One volunteer excitedly shared how rich an experience he had working and talking with those from here and abroad. A local resident shared how the time together moved her and how the lodge would carry their memory in it. The sharing was emotionally reinforcing, but it was the Elder who brought us into a greater and more profound sense of what we had done. The Elder quietly asked if he might share a few words. Then the diminutive man, worn with age, stepped forward and spoke.

"'Your coming has meant much to us,' he said. 'We see and feel your care. You came from all different places and joined us.' At this point, he began to sob. 'We want to thank you! Please, I need to say some things, so I will pray a prayer in my native tongue.'

"The Elder prayed in a language none of us could understand. As tears welled up in his eyes and his faltering words, unrecognizable, arose from the depths of his heart, we listened in silence.

"The sounds of his words wrapped themselves around us, seeming to weave patterns inside our bodies. Suddenly, his words dove into the depths of our hearts, filling us with emotion. Together, we stood transfixed in empathy. The words of the Elder's staccato prayer were punctuated by a growing wave of sobs. It was like the first drop of rain before the clouds released the multitudes. Soon the entire group joined in the chorus of sobs. Our faces glistening with tears, together we felt that we were not afraid and that we were not alone—we were one.

"We all knew that the Elder's tears lamented a critically wounded history. They were met with our tears, and we as one family could be reunited with God's tears. We, as one family, cried in release, relief, and the joy of our homecoming. In those moments, we clearly felt that we stood as one family in the embrace of healing love."

The Grandfather paused.

"Hernando and Joseph," he suddenly addressed the two. "You don't understand this, but you are part of history. There have been many hurts given between the fair-skinned peoples of the world and the people with more pigment in their skin. There have been misguided notions of superiority; there have been selfishness and exploitation; retaliation and retribution, as well as sincere love and efforts to help. I hope you will both choose a better future, not only for yourselves but to redeem history and give humanity a chance at peace. After all, world peace begins in each human heart."

The Grandfather rose. "I need help bringing out the treats and snacks I have for all of you today." He waved off

Juan and Chrissy as they moved to get to their feet. "Joseph and Hernando, please come with me to the kitchen and help me serve your fellow students, won't you?"

A little sheepishly, Joseph and Hernando got to their feet to help the Grandfather. Their classmates very graciously thanked them as they passed out the treats, making sure each felt accepted and appreciated. Embarrassed, Joseph and Hernando helped each other gather up the trays and extra cups and took them into the kitchen. There was silence, and the boys came peaceably out of the kitchen area to where the class was starting to file out.

Mr. Bennet stood back.

"Thanks," he said to the Grandfather. "Sometimes, these teenage boys are hard to handle. The last thing I want to do is suspend either of those boys. Their grades are teetering on the edge as it is."

"Perhaps they learned their lesson," suggested the Grandfather. "At least, I hope so."

"I hope so, too," said Mr. Bennet. "I didn't hear any cups breaking when they were alone in the kitchen! Well,

I'd better catch up with them now to make sure the peace treaty holds."

Part IV: Service as a Force for Peace: Healing and Reconciliation to Resolve Resentment

Chapter 15: "This Is Why I Hate You"

"It is easy to be friendly to one's friends but to befriend the one who regards himself as your enemy is the quintessence of true religion. The other is mere business."
Mohandas K. Gandhi

Mr. Bennet told Hernando and Joseph that he would not report their fight to the principal this time since they had shown some cooperation afterward at the Grandfather's. Neither of them had been physically hurt during the fracas, and there had been no property damage. They had behaved themselves on the walk back to school as well.

"I hope I'm doing the right thing," Mr. Bennet sighed to the Grandfather as the students milled around the refreshment tables in the Grandfather's yard and garden during the next class. "I don't want to break down discipline, make the kids think they can get away with things. Still, these guys are going to be graduating next year. I want them to learn how to solve things in real-time, not rely on a principal or boss to do it for them."

The Grandfather nodded. "I've geared today's story toward the theme of reconciliation. Let's see if that does some good."

The truce between Hernando and Joseph was clearly an uneasy one. The Grandfather noticed that they sat far apart from one another and that the other students were uncomfortable around them too, straining to make casual, natural conversation when either gravitated toward a knot of them. What was more, any time Hernando and Joseph drifted into one another's orbit, everyone tensed up.

The Grandfather nodded to himself. Acrimony, resentment, and fighting had a ripple effect. No one wanted to be around such goings-on. The only antidote he had ever seen was consciously and openly addressing the issues in the spirit of service. He's seen it work on the macro level. Would it work on the micro-level?

Juan and Chrissy played and sang a pretty duet. Their singing and playing seemed a bit strained with the situation. The Grandfather assumed his place for speaking on a grassy knoll, feeling burdened yet hopeful.

"Good afternoon, my friends," he said after the song. "Welcome, one and all. Now, tell me, how would you like to do a service project with two people whose first conversation together involved one of them saying to the other: 'I hate you and all your kind, and I'll tell you why? And mind you, these were RYS volunteers who were supposed to be practicing service and who were going to show the world how love was the answer to all problems!"

The students let out a gust of laughter, and both Joseph and Hernando looked relieved, as if glad to hear that other people had problems with bad feelings too.

"Well, even people with high ideals have their issues, and the RYS volunteers were no exception. Neither am I; neither is anyone. We all carry our hatred, prejudices, and misconceptions about other people. Don't we?"

His provocative pause elicited slow, quiet nods from many of the students. Hernando's brow cleared, as did Joseph's.

"One way our staff worked to deal with those unresolved issues and attitudes was to put together, as roommates, volunteers from nations or cultures that held grudges against each other. In a close living situation, each person would find his or her presumptions and prejudices challenged as they encountered someone from a hated group as a human individual. When those participants made it through the program, they were sure to have learned some valuable life lessons. Naturally, the first pair of roommates we selected were Ezra and Bilal. Bilal was the one who had told Ezra that he hated him and all he stood for. Not the best beginning for a friendship, was it?"

The students laughed uneasily.

"Their problems had a history, as so many such problems do. One seemingly unsolvable situation in our world is the entangled relationships of people living in and around the 'Holy Land'. In this region, tension, resentment, and hatred appear to be as long-lasting as subarctic permafrost. When a spike in the emotional temperature occurs, some of the frosts melts, and anger seeps out, leaving a muddy, sticky, and at times, fatal pathway.

"Resentment is like a knot that keeps us tied to a prison. It is a key factor of why the Middle Eastern region seems stuck in a recurring pattern of violence and distrust. History is full of injustice and offers many excuses for people to resent others. As individuals, families, and even nations, we remain prisoners to resentment till we unknot it from our hearts. Only one force is strong enough to untie the knot of resentment, and that is the power of love.

"The RYS came to Rome from 40 nations, 120 volunteers strong. We were there to help construct a training and distribution center for Northern African immigrants. Once completed, these buildings would be run by Catholic organizations. They would feed, clothe, and train immigrants in employable skills. In addition to the anticipated physical work, we were hoping that our living, working, and sharing together would model to a skeptical world the positive impact religious cooperation can achieve.

"Our volunteers included some who came from ethnic, national, and religious backgrounds that shared a long history of animosity. Among us were black and white South Africans, Israeli Jews and Palestinian Arabs, Hindus from India, and Muslims from Pakistan. We typically brought with us a set of attitudes and stereotypes that our forthcoming experiences would challenge. For us, these experiences were like receiving a new pair of glasses, offering a fresh, clearer perspective on life and the people who enrich it.

"All the volunteers anticipated making good friends during our seven weeks together. We looked forward to sharing meals, work, conversations, cultural insights, and, hopefully, lots of laughter. We were going to be living close together, so it was important to establish positive relationships.

"Ezra, an Israeli Jew, and Bilal, a Muslim from Jordan, were both outstanding volunteers with strong academic and social service backgrounds. Yet creating a friendship between them was challenging.

"At one of the first meals, Ezra sat next to Bilal with a plate full of food. Ezra posed a series of questions and inquiries to Bilal in hopes of striking up a conversation. Bilal's response to each question was terse and razor-sharp. Ezra's attempts at establishing a conversation were getting nowhere fast. Eventually, he reached a point of frustration and asked Bilal point-blank, 'Do you hate me?' Bilal unabashedly responded, 'Yes, I do hate you, and I hate all your kind, and I'll tell you why.'

"For nearly an hour, Bilal went on to explain with great emotion his resentment toward Israel, the Jews, and the current political situation. Bilal's Palestinian parents had left Israel during a time of conflict and had never returned to their childhood homes. As a family living in Jordan, they carried the weight of that loss deep in their hearts.

"To Bilal, Ezra represented all the people and things he had grown to resent. This scene in the dining room was a reminder that substantial issues needed to be worked on if our group was to approach the level of understanding and cooperation we idealistically sought.

"Yet an interesting process of change took place at our worksite over the weeks together. The physical construction at our worksite developed in stages but so did our ways of seeing each other.

"'Rome in the summer is fit only for tourists and dogs,' say some Romans as they exit the city during the summer. At our worksites, the heat knew no favorites. The physical labor of moving wheelbarrows of dirt, passing cinder blocks, mixing cement, and doing the numerous tasks needed to construct a small building, was made harder on account of the heat. Compounding these difficulties was our general lack of building experience.

"During the first work week, we shared various aches, pains, and difficulties. Yet, because we were going through these things together, they seemed a bit more manageable. The construction site on our arrival was simply a foundation. As the structure took shape and grew, so did our confidence. While working together, we drew encouragement from each other and became increasingly aware of a growing personal satisfaction that came from a sense of accomplishment.

"Daily, the level of cooperation grew despite difficulties with language and vast cultural and religious differences. For many women, this was the first opportunity to use a variety of tools and do manual work for an extended period. Some struggled and just did what they could, but others took on all challengers to see who could do the job the best.

"Some of our young men initially looked at manual labor as something only the poor in their country did. It was

confronting to have to 'step down' and do such lowly work. Yet, after investing their own sweat and seeing the result, they began to understand the importance of manual labor. Our eyes were beginning to see through new glasses and recognize the sacrifice laborers made daily to provide food for their families.

"I remember asking Bilal what he thought about the work he was doing, and he gave a very deep and interesting response. 'Work is like worshiping God,' he said, 'When I hammer this wood and fix this building, I am worshiping God with my actions.'

"During our time together, we found plenty of time to laugh and gently poke fun at each other. Each of us understood that, as volunteers, we left behind family, friends, and comforts. If you looked at us gathered together, it was as if representatives from all over the world had been brought to this place to share the joy and satisfaction of the moment.

"Following the conclusion of our work, we set aside a time for reflection in Assisi, the city of St. Francis. We arrived at the time of the annual pilgrimage and asked a local Franciscan priest if it was appropriate for our interreligious group to participate. The kindly priest offered us some insight about St. Francis that made us feel at home.

"'St. Francis is remembered for the beautiful simplicity of his faith. His spirit and example have moved many to seek God while encouraging the church to go back to its roots. Francis saw God in all people, and this motivated him to reach out and promote understanding between people of different religions. He journeyed to the

Holy Land and met with the Sultan, who was a Muslim. He respectfully shared his faith with the Sultan and listened to the Sultan as he shared his. His exceptional concern was aimed at helping to bring about a better relationship between Muslims and Christians.'

"It seemed we were in the right place at the right time. The priest said, 'Francis longed for the day when all humanity would live together as one family, God's family. Your group represents the fruit of St. Francis's prayers, as he so much wanted to see this beautiful respect between those who love God. Please join the pilgrimage.'

"While devout Catholics from far and near gathered to start the pilgrimage, they were joined by our young ambassadors from each of the world's religions. Muslim, Sikh, Jain, Jew, Protestant, Hindu, Buddhist, Unificationist, Parsi, Copt, and Roman Catholic reverently joined the pilgrimage. Candles in hand, we walked the narrow, hilly streets of the medieval city. It was a deeply moving experience for all who took part.

"On concluding the pilgrimage, we meandered to the village plaza. Feeling the spirit, Rev. Alan Celestine, an African American minister, started singing the upbeat hymn, 'We are the Children of the Living God'. We started dancing and singing along, and the excitement pulled in local onlookers. When the song concluded, we began to jump up and down, clapping and smiling, feeling an exhilarating peace. This was clearly a scene that would have moved the heart of St. Francis. Perhaps his spirit was there, dancing and singing with us.

"After things quieted down that evening, Ezra pulled me aside to have a conversation.

"'You must know that Bilal and I have gone through a lot on this project. We both came because we wanted to serve people who needed help. By joining this special work to help the refugees, we managed to see and appreciate something good in each other. We went through challenges, hardships, and fun together, and that brought us closer. Recently, we were able to have some really deep conversations that have helped us both.'

"After pausing a few moments, Ezra continued, 'Back home, we live and interact with our own kind. We see others, but it is almost like they exist in a parallel universe. During this program and on the pilgrimage, we walked, worked, shared, and prayed together. We now have some of the same friends. With all our differences, we recognize that what we share is what is most important. We love our families; we worship God; and we work to make the world a little better. We became friends; better yet, we became brothers.'

"All I could do was nod and smile. Ezra and Bilal recognized they were united as members of God's great family. This is the essence from which peace can grow, and it is the foundation of true religion."

After the talk, the students worked together to bring leftover food, used and unused dishes, and silverware to the Grandfather's kitchen. Then there was a gasp and a moment of silence when Hernando and Joseph both reached to lift up a blue-and-white-cooler still full of unopened bottles of spring water.

"I can handle it alone," said Joseph, waving Hernando off.

"So can I," said Hernando, beginning to bristle. "I can lift it by myself."

"Okay," said Joseph, seemingly with a change of heart. "I'm sure you can. But it would be easier if we carried it together."

Hernando nodded slowly. "Yeah," he admitted.

Each boy grabbed a handle, and together, they carried the heavy cooler toward the Grandfather's kitchen.

Joseph and Hernando passed Mr. Bennet and the Grandfather while hauling the heavy cooler together. The young men glanced defensively at the two older men.

The Grandfather concentrated on looking very innocent while Mr. Bennet ducked his head to hide his smile.

Chapter 16: The Beautiful Power of the International Bridge of Love

"Your living is determined not so much by what life brings to you as by the attitude you bring to life; not so much by what happens to you as by the way your mind looks at what happens."

Kahlil Gibran

Rumors circulated a few days before the next class that the Grandfather was in the hospital. The students were highly alarmed. Juan and Chrissy waylaid Mr. Bennet in the hallway.

"What happened to the Grandfather?" Juan queried.

Mr. Bennet looked distressed. "Well, he had some dental work done, and unfortunately, he is on a blood thinner for heart issues. He started bleeding profusely at home. It's fortunate one of his neighbors dropped by to leave off some treats for our class. He lost some blood. They took him to the hospital, and his doctor wants him to stay a few days."

"Oh, no!" said Chrissy. "That sounds serious!"

"He's going to be all right, I hear. So this week, we will have a planning session for our project instead of going to the Grandfather's."

Chrissy cried, "We should visit him in the hospital!"

Mr. Bennet looked weary. "Chrissy, it's too much, arranging transportation and insurance for the whole class. This project and the visits to the Grandfather are already quite experimental for this school. I'm afraid I have to ask you to visit the Grandfather on your own time, providing your own transportation."

Chrissy looked at Juan desperately.

"Well, Kyle can drive," Juan said, unable to resist the plea in her eyes.

"Kyle doesn't have a car," Chrissy pointed out.

They both avoided meeting Mr. Bennet's eyes, but he got the message. He sighed.

"You can use my car if you go after school and get back by 5:30 or 6:00. I've got to stay and grade some tests. Only you three go—I don't want twenty teenagers packed in my car. And make sure Kyle stays on the right side of the speed limit."

"You've got it!" said Juan, and he and Chrissy ran down the hall to find Kyle.

"No running in the halls," said Mr. Bennet sternly, but Juan and Chrissy were already out of earshot.

Aside from some trouble finding a parking place near the hospital, the trio made its way to the Grandfather's bedside in record time after school.

He was asleep when they arrived, and he looked ten years older. Chrissy and Juan hesitated, whispering together as to whether they should just leave and let the Grandfather rest.

"Hi, Grandfather!" said Kyle, sauntering up to the bed brazenly. "How about a high five?"

The Grandfather's blue eyes whipped open, and he stared uncomprehendingly for a moment. Then he broke into a grin.

"You three," he murmured. "You are my best loyalists."

"How do you feel, Grandfather?" asked Chrissy solicitously, taking the Grandfather's hand.

"Much better at the sight of your young faces."

"Oh, good!" said Chrissy.

Kyle stood grinning at the foot of the Grandfather's bed, and Juan took possession of the Grandfather's other hand.

"So you had some dental work done," encouraged Juan gently. The Grandfather nodded.

"Was it like in the Philippines?" asked Kyle. "Where they just pulled people's teeth out?"

"No, Kyle," smiled the Grandfather. "It was a dental bridge, very complex and well done. I neglected to mention my blood thinners to the dentist. But I've been thinking of the Philippines, Kyle, and how little they had of the kind of fine treatment I received. We actually built a bridge there — the kind that goes over water — in the same village where we had our Dental Day."

"Would you mind telling us about it?" asked Chrissy. Her eyes met Juan's. He nodded, affirming that they both thought the best thing for the Grandfather might be to tell them a story.

They were right. As he sat up and began speaking, the Grandfather's face lit up, and he looked younger. He seemed to gain vigor as he spoke.

"I have seen and experienced the healing and reconciliation that can take place between perceived enemies once a bridge — psychological or physical — is built. It is powerful and life-changing. My hope is that we all can become forces of healing and reconciliation in our families, our communities, our nation, and wherever we go.

"Can you imagine investing six weeks of your time working, sharing meals, and living side-by-side with 40 people from backgrounds reflecting a microcosm of the world? Coworkers included a Sikh graduate student, a Turkish engineer, an Australian surfer, a Palestinian Muslim scholar, and an African Christian college student. There was also a vocal Sri Lankan activist, a compassionate Hindu social worker, a Unification Church seminarian, and a dynamic Israeli grad student.

"In July 1986, with the excitement of the nonviolent People Power Revolution still fresh in everyone's mind, we convened. Then we had to cope with the arrival of an unwelcome visitor—a powerful typhoon!

"The typhoon struck at the heart of the Philippines, unleashing killer winds, torrential rain, and massive flooding. We were well-sheltered, but it would not take long for us to discover some of the devastation wrought by the storm. Once the storm winds had subsided, we traveled into Manila for a special face-to-face meeting with the new president, Mrs. Cory Aquino. Packed into a bus, we made the exceptionally slow journey to the presidential residence, as floodwaters had covered much of the low-lying areas. Peering through bus windows while riding through certain neighborhoods, we were exposed to a level of poverty many of us had never seen.

"Those images of poverty faded from our memory when we were welcomed at the presidential residence by the gracious president. With genuine warmth, the president offered us her attention while personally encouraging many of us. In front of the media's cameras, she thanked us for coming to serve her country 'with a heart of kindness and concern'. We remembered her words as inspiration when we faced some of the challenges that lay ahead.

"When we returned to our bus and drove through the flooded regions, we were again visually reminded of the difficulties that so many of the citizens of this country faced.

"As I've mentioned before, Das Marinas, which is a coastal community, had recently gone through an upheaval, receiving many new residents. Their families had been forcibly removed from poorer sections of Manila by the previous administration.

"In Das Marinas, Muslims had settled on one side of a stream while the larger Christian population occupied housing on the other side. The Muslims and Christians were not openly hostile, but their relations brimmed with strong undercurrents of distrust. It felt to us that a common purpose was needed in Das Marinas to pull the divided community together. We decided to build a bridge across the stream in close cooperation with engineering students and faculty from the local campus of the Technical University of the Philippines (TUP).

"One thing we noticed while walking the narrow neighborhood streets was clusters of undernourished children playing group games with makeshift balls. It appeared that the children were constantly discovering ways to play, using whatever could be found or imagined.

Despite the weight of poverty, laughter played a part in most people's days.

"Certain inevitable challenges arose within our diverse community. Our volunteers hailed from a wide variety of cultural, religious, ethnic, economic, and educational backgrounds. We arrived in the Philippines with different mindsets and attitudes, and soon discovered that we could easily differ in the ways we did things.

"Keeping time was one clear example. Being on time meant something quite different for the English and Swiss participants than it did for the Nigerians and Brazilians. We often struggled to find a consensus on what 'on time' meant!

"Another experience in mixing cultural norms came as we offered greetings to people. A Venezuelan man would typically greet both men and women with a kiss on both cheeks. For Muslim women, receiving a kiss from an unrelated male was a big shock. It was prohibited. Bows were given to people who offered outstretched hands, and hugs were given to those that preferred bows. We had to learn from each other.

"Though our cultural upbringings differed, we shared one great unifying element—our desire to serve. Having something important to work for allowed us to see beyond many cultural challenges.

"The labor we were tasked with was largely done by hand under a severe tropical sun. The cheerful and diligent example of the engineering students helped to neutralize most of our complaints. These university representatives provided skills, energy, smiles, and encouragement to each of us. We were proud to be their friends.

"As we dug, mixed cement, and relayed dirt and bricks while sharing conversation and songs, the construction site increasingly became a source of entertainment for the local children. Initially, curious children from the Christian sector came to watch. Before long, the children from the Muslim sector began to join in. Both Muslim and Christian children were filled with equal curiosity. In addition, the situation provided an opportunity for them to get to know children whom they had not known very well before.

"Within days, women from both sides of the stream came to our worksite, in part searching for their children but also to satisfy their own curiosity. After seeing how intensely we were laboring, they quickly decided to get involved by bringing drinks to quench our thirst. The women also offered words of encouragement and their simple laughter, which was a good way to lift our hearts.

"Some of the men were puzzled to understand why we were there. They questioned why a young doctor from the poor nation of Bangladesh, for example, had come to Das Marinas, as there was so much work to do back at his home. It was hard for some to imagine foreigners coming to the Philippines to do hard labor instead of enjoying its beaches and other attractions. With a mixture of paternal care and macho pride, they finally arrived at the consensus that we were probably in the community for the right reasons. It was at this point that men from both the Christian and Muslim sectors of the community began to grab shovels and placed themselves in the middle of the construction efforts.

One representative citizen said, 'This is our community, and we want to help.'

"Now, whole families from both the Christian and Muslim sectors of the community were meeting at our construction site. The bridge became our shared goal. Our combined efforts were creating a sense of solidarity. One of our Philippine RYS members, Elizabeth Mendoza, shared that this little bridge built by these many hands was truly 'The International Bridge of Love.' Soon a song was written about it, and many of us learned to sing it.

"In time, the work was complete. We decided that the bridge deserved a show of color. We painted it with yellow and black paint. That way, it was properly dressed for its inauguration.

"The inauguration of the bridge was a major event. The Roman Catholic bishop, the local imam, the governor, and RYS Director Rev. Hose were all part of the ribbon-cutting ceremony. Many hundreds of residents came to share in the festivities.

"Everyone was celebrating. Rev. David Hose, a generous man, took nearly all the personal money he had brought with him and purchased every ice cream cup and cone available from the local shops. We happily distributed the ice cream to the hundreds of children and adults who gathered for the ribbon-cutting ceremony.

"The air was electric with the excitement of the crowd as we inched closer to the formal ceremony. Gathered at the front entrance to the bridge were the spiritual and secular leaders of the community. Crowds gathered close to the bishop who was dressed in his traditional robes and offered paternal smiles to the religiously diverse audience. The Imam was a humble co-celebrant. The governor emanated the warm friendliness that political leaders often master.

"The recently divided community was crowding together as one body—happy, proud, and open to a brighter future. As the ribbon fell away and slowly dropped to the ground, so also, it seemed, had the barriers that divided the community. We were wrapped in an overwhelming sense of accomplishment.

"The bridge was an asset to the community. The children and the general population gained easier access to the school and the local markets. More children would be able to continue their schooling as a result.

"However, something less visible had also taken place during our month in Das Marinas. A divided community was beginning to share respect and trust as neighbors saw each other with new eyes. We, a motley group of young adults, representatives of the religions and nations of the world, had helped achieve this metaphysical healing. Such was the legacy of the International Bridge of Love."

Chrissy had tears in her eyes. The Grandfather patted her hand.

"You three are a little younger than those who were on this adventure, but you have much of the same passion for life. You are also seekers, striving to fulfill some special purpose. In so many ways, you are like those who went to the International Bridge of Love project. I see in your faces a longing to be of help and to serve those in need. You still are searching for the confidence you need to do what you are called to do. When you are young, it is hard to understand your value and your potential to transform people's lives, but you have both, just as the RYS volunteers did.

"Remember that each of us is destined to meet with struggles. We all get knocked down, some more often than others. How we get back up is so important. As Kahil Gibran said, 'Your living is determined not so much by what life brings to you as by the attitude you bring to life; not so much by what happens to you as by the way your mind looks at what happens.' These are wise thoughts to carry with us on our journey. Can we use our struggles to gain insights, confidence, determination? That is our choice.

"Some problems may seem intractable. Religious conflict, for example, is a painful reality in parts of our world, but our seekers saw a different reality: Muslims and Christians working and sharing together to make life better for a community. They were joined by representatives of every religion and culture. It seems so simple, but it is positively revolutionary. The barriers our hearts, minds, and attitudes create can melt away through the power of love and service. You do not read that in the headlines of our newspapers, but that is where it belongs.

"I am incredibly happy you chose to visit tonight. Please, if you take just one thing from our time together, consider this: 'Our life is the gift we have been given, and we learn through our service how best to give it.'"

The trio stood silently, absorbing the Grandfather's words. Then Chrissy leaned over and kissed him on the forehead.

"Get well, Grandpa," she said. "Please."

He smiled. "I will. For you dear young people, I will."

Chapter 17: My African Sister

"The best way to get rid of an enemy is to make him into a friend."

Abraham Lincoln

The Grandfather was back! He had received excellent care at the hospital and had gained ground quickly. With adjustments to his medications and the help of his neighbors, he was doing well and was bright-eyed once again.

In fact, the tables full of food were almost creaking under the weight of the hearty and nutritious dishes his neighbors had showered on the Grandfather.

Juan took his guitar out and tuned it as the gathered group started to settle down. He had an acute sense of what kind of music would help set the stage for the Grandfather to begin sharing. He played a lively tune that had, in the middle of it, a sense of loss as the music slowed down and grew sorrowful before it picked up again. He found that middle part hard to get through.

The Grandfather's hospitalization had hit a little too close to home for Juan. It had reminded him of the last few days of his father's life. He caught the Grandfather's bright glance of encouragement and made it through the sad part of the song. As the notes rose in a triumphant pattern, the theme ascending over loss and adversity, so did Juan's spirits. He finished with a flourish, enjoyed the applause, and nodded to the Grandfather as he lifted his guitar strap and sat down in the front row.

Sometimes the Grandfather stood to speak, but this day he gratefully sank into one of the living room chairs that Joseph and Hernando had toted out onto the lawn.

The Grandfather asked his audience, "Have you ever been misjudged because a person did not take the time or effort to get to know you? Has anyone ever judged you unfairly?"

Many of the students hung their heads in sadness. High school was a morass of cliques. People were often judged and discarded because of clothing they wore, a careless word, text or post, or a friendship with someone who was "out".

"Have you had friends that were judged based on their race, nationality, educational background, looks, or social standing? How did you feel about that? I imagine it would make any of us sad, angry, and disappointed. Do you think that it is possible that we, at times, can make similar mistaken judgments?

"Too often, we fall short of doing the hard work needed to get to know and understand a person. This is a human shortcoming and probably one that each of us shares. It is much simpler and easier to place people in categories and make generalized judgments and assumptions.

"At times, our assumptions are confirmed, but, like any judgement, they may be wrong. Assumptions can be dangerous. They can have us believing in a fiction, a lie, a misunderstanding. It takes humility and strength of character to back away from old attitudes and look at a person with fresh eyes and an open heart.

"Abraham Lincoln understood this and said: 'The best way to get rid of an enemy is to make him into a friend.' This is not an easy challenge, but it is a noble one. In this story, we will see what happens when people go beyond their assumptions and grow to understand the uniqueness of each one of us. We will see an enemy become a friend.

"Crucial and important events often escape the headlines. Many significant events take place in various sectors, yet often, the most significant developments are achieved quietly, through good relationships shaped by trust and care.

"Two participants on the RYS project in Italy accomplished something during a summer of service that offers useful insights into how to build trust and respect and how to destroy boundaries between antagonists.

"Although they both came from the same continent, Africa, it seemed like Christine from South Africa, and Samuel from Ethiopia were from two different worlds. To gain a clearer sense of the struggles and attitudes that Samuel and Christine encountered, it helps to know the social and political situation that they lived in.

"In the 1980s, South Africa was governed under a racial policy known as apartheid. Apartheid rule force-fed a process of de-personalization and dehumanization. People were lumped into racial categories. The hard work of differentiating one person from another, discovering uniqueness, and encouraging development was simply ignored.

"On a personal level, apartheid ripped and tore the heart, mind, and soul. It did this in a blatant way to black, colored, and Indian South Africans, but it also worked in a more subtle way on the white population. Many of the white South Africans were losing their souls little by little as an inevitable result of voicelessly standing by and observing the defenseless be beaten and abused. This was a system that robbed some more than others, but it took from all.

"This system faced a growing tide of resistance from within the nation and from the international community. Opposition to the government policy of apartheid developed, and eventually, it was dismantled. From today's perspective, that achievement seems to have been inevitable, but when Christine met Samuel, it was a dream that only the brave believed in.

"You can imagine how Africans from Ghana, Angola, or Ethiopia felt about apartheid. They held deep feelings of anger and disgust toward the system and toward white South Africans, lumping them all into the single category of the oppressor.

"Native Americans offer us a wise insight that can help us in our quest to make better relationships. A Sioux elder suggested to a young man full of accusations and premature judgments that it is important to walk a mile in someone else's moccasins before judging him. This sage advice remains important for all of us. The story of Samuel and Christine offers us a chance to see what happens when we have the patience to walk that mile in the other person's shoes.

"Dr. Christine Landmann was born white, a woman, and a South African. She received a very good education. She had an interest in world religions and happened to like people of all races and cultures in her quiet, intellectual way. Christine went to Rome on the RYS project, hoping to learn about different religions and, in the process, offered her help in the construction of a shelter for the homeless.

"Samuel was born in Ethiopia. His dark skin and long, thin frame were carried with strength and dignity. By faith, he was a Copt whose ancient church had deep roots in the early days of Christianity. In his actions, he displayed a strong but warm character that put people at ease.

"Early in our project, at a time when we were just starting to get to know one another, Samuel said of Christine: "I don't care what she does or what she thinks. I

will never consider her an African."

"Our group initially stayed at the home of the Oblate Sisters in an area of Rome where large numbers of North African refugees lived and struggled. For five weeks, we labored together constructing floors, walls, and the ceiling of a building next to the home of the Sisters. This new building was to be used to feed, bathe, and clothe hundreds of street people and those living on the margins.

"Both Samuel and Christine worked day after day, moving piles of sand, digging foundations, laying bricks, mixing cement, and smoothing surfaces while bending and straining their backs and muscles. The heat from the sun was impartial; it burned intensely on us all. Fair, light, white Christine was one of the quickest to burn. Samuel's skin did not suffer the same fate.

"Thirst, pain, sweat, pushing through obstacles, and swaggering after accomplishments were daily rituals at the worksite. These things helped give us a common point of reference. Yet, some community members pulled together more easily than others. Christine was not one of those. Instead of quick acceptance, she found herself being studied under watchful eyes, even though she was laboring like she never had before. How many well-educated, white, South African ladies spent their days shoveling dirt and mixing cement? Back home, that kind of hard labor was strictly the work of the blacks or the coloreds, as they were called.

"The challenge was hard for Christine both physically and emotionally, since by nature she clearly preferred the library to the construction site. Yet, as time passed, she got better at work, and she hung on till the end.

"Our shared experiences over five full weeks did something to each of us. We could begin to strongly identify with each other and take pride in what we as a group had accomplished. If we had been actors in a drama, the audience would have seen a widely diverse group — racially, ethnically, religiously, educationally, and socially different. In the beginning of the story, there was a stiffness in some of the actors as they struggled on the set, each not quite knowing how to relate to the others and to the broader storyline. In this drama, as time passed, the opening atmosphere of anxious curiosity, uncertainty, and insecurity was gradually transformed. We, as the actors, began to sense the interweaving of our parts and could more easily give impromptu performances that resulted in spontaneous moments of joy.

"We were clearly writing our own lines. We got away from the scripts that we had been reading for so many years and offered our new friends pieces of ourselves that no audience had ever been exposed to.

"Respect is often produced when we appreciate what another has done or is doing. When we look around at our community and see something bold, challenging, and good, it's natural to develop mutual respect. Respect is not a gender thing, nor a color thing; it is simply a human thing. When we begin to respect others, we can start to find common ground. This is what happened between Samuel and Christine.

"Samuel and Christine had some opportunities to talk and share while they were at the worksite. Those occasions multiplied as we neared the end of the project. During the closing days of our program, we gathered and shared our stories. Some were deeply meaningful, whereas others were just rip-roaring hilarious.

Our thoughts and feelings became ever more transparent as we got closer to our time of departure.

"On the closing day of the work, Samuel, whose tall, lean frame towered over Christine, came close to Christine. Opening his arms and offering Christine a large embrace, he said, 'Christine, you are my African sister.' Christine looked up at Samuel with a warm smile of appreciation and whispered, 'My brother.'"

The Grandfather paused to let the feeling of reconciliation and healing sink in. "This is one example of how the power of love can help us work through the pain needed for healing and reconciliation," he said. Then he turned and said softly,

"Juan?"

Juan reached for his guitar, thinking the Grandfather wanted him to play a closing song. With the Grandfather's soft, sad little smile, Juan realized what was needed. He rose and offered his arm to the Grandfather, taking much of the old man's weight upon himself so the Grandfather could stand. Chrissy bolted to her feet to support the Grandfather's other arm. As they gently helped the Grandfather toward his home, they heard the class burst into applause, the way an audience did when a sports figure arose from an injury to limp off the field.

Credit: This story was first published in Dialogue & Alliance, Vol. 24, No. 1, Spring-Summer 2010 http://upf.org/upf-news/141-africa-middle-east/3148-dialogue-a-alliance-voices-of-peace-in-africa

Chapter 18: God Bless the English?

"Without forgiveness, life is governed by ... an endless cycle
of resentment and retaliation."
Roberto Assagioli

Juan and Chrissy got permission from Mr. Bennet to leave class early to head to the Grandfather's home to help make some preparations. They talked with the Grandfather to get a sense of his energy levels, which were improving but still delicate, and to ascertain what kind of story they would hear that day. Responsibility for the music at the gatherings had been left up to the pair. They increasingly enjoyed the challenge of trying to create a musical canvas to go along with the tales. They enjoyed the freedom and creativity that was offered and were gaining insights into how to move people into a certain frame of mind.

The Grandfather enjoyed the opportunity to preview his storytelling to Juan and Chrissy by giving a short story summary and sharing what message he hoped the story would convey. Sometimes Juan offered a few comments and ventured an occasional suggestion. On such occasions, the Grandfather would usually offer a nod of appreciation. With each meeting, they learned ways to improve their communication with each other and with those coming to the sessions. Both Juan and the Grandfather took great personal satisfaction from their growing relationship.

Grandfather finished his personal greetings to those in the room and polished off his coffee while Juan was finishing his second song. The older man found his way to his usual speaking area, and when the restless energy started to settle, he thanked all of them for coming. He ignored the chair Joseph and Hernando had brought out on the lawn, but he thanked them for bringing it.

"I'll see how long I can go without it," he said, smiling at the pair, who were sitting next to one another. "Your efforts were not in vain. I know it's there if I need it.

"Today, I am a bit nervous as I will read you a poem written soon after walking the streets in Belfast, Ireland. My walks took me through areas that had known the blast of bombs. Bombs indiscriminately ripped apart the flesh of people of all ages. The tears of widows, mothers, brothers, and sisters had filled these streets during the so-called time of the troubles. These written words were born in a burst of raw emotion. I put them on paper, as the emotions inside me needed some way to find expression.

"Since many of you may not be not familiar with the history that is the background of this story, let me share some things about the not-too-distant history of Belfast and the time of the troubles.

"The land in the north of Ireland has a history as sad as the countryside is beautiful. Contested along sectarian lines, in the decades following the formation of the Republic of Ireland, the region harbored some of the bloodiest acts of terror and retaliation of the 20th century. 'Bloody' Belfast was a descriptive headline that too often

announced another act of violence costing life and limb. Those aligned with the Protestants, who consider themselves British, and those aligned with the Catholics, who consider themselves Irish, found different avenues to combat each other. The British had intervened at times, and bloodshed had followed. It seemed that there was no way to end the cycle of violence.

"What results can be hoped for if some people are determined to bring about change while others are equally determined to protect the status quo, and both sides have adherents willing to kill to get their way? This was the dilemma that was faced by the people of Northern Ireland, and it was a recipe for trouble and prolonged strife.

"Fortunately, at some point, people can become exhausted by the hatred and violence and seek more humane approaches to problem-solving. At such a time, political leaders can help break deadlocks between those that seem to have irreconcilable differences. Yet, more often, it is the ordinary people: widows, grieving mothers, those with hearts that yearn for peace and reconciliation who lead the way.

"On my first day in Belfast, I saw a rather pretty city with lots of flowers and greenery. This was different from the image presented by the international media, which often focused on carnage left after a bomb blast. As a newcomer to Belfast, I needed to discover the city through my own eyes and talk to local people. The best way for me to do this was by walking the streets.

"The cool weather encouraged walking. Sauntering down Antrim Road, I stood in front of the Europa Hotel where we stayed and lumbered past the Orange Order Headquarters, which was boarded up with plywood, like some other targetable buildings. With shops, pedestrians, and mothers walking their children, it was an ordinary day. Some places were harder to digest. I walked down Shankill Road, the scene of unspeakable atrocities, and it stirred up emotions that are difficult to describe in words.

"In the decades that have passed, one central realization remains: the stinging power of resentment can kill even the innocent. The Belfast experience pushed me to reexamine my own faith in the power of love. If I were a grieving mother, could I forgive my child's killers? If I were shut out of opportunities and doors were closed on my children, could I look at the persecutors with a clear heart rather than a clenched fist?

"Life often makes unfair demands on each of us. It is hard to tell the grieving mother to hold on to love. Yet, I know for myself, if I let go of love, the currents of life will pull me down, down to a place where no one should go. Many turn to a higher power during such difficulties. In that higher power, they find a source of love, one where a curative to resentment resides.

"I wrote a few lines down on paper when I came back to my room that September day. I had paused for a time to watch a small band of young children freely playing in and near the street where I stood. I wondered if a new way of thinking and behaving would ever wrest these children from cycles of fear and resentment.

For the Children of Belfast

Ye lost ones, those who shatter guiltless bones,
Breaking bodies, cruelly crushing as with a sharp stone.
Discerning not the essence of victims left behind.
Categorizing others the Enemy, without remorse to remind.

With blasting sounds and splinters that rip,
Terror holding others in a tight fatal grip.

Senselessly serving as a harbinger of hate,
Tallying grim satisfaction over other people's fate.

Resentment chokes dry the compassion of your heart,
While you stand, willing agent, and do your vicious part.
Perpetuating violence on violence, no end in sight,
Unless resentment is liberated and given a final respite.

What force could disarm the thrice-violent men?
To self, country, and those stricken suddenly dead,
Is there a source that is greater than violence and hate?
'True love,' you say with the patience of a saint.

Ancient wisdom renders in troubled times a light,
Ways to change injustices from deathly wrong to right.
Souls freed from resentment's wounds thrust so deep,
Lips that offer forgiveness for the hurts they weep.

Liberation, oh, liberation is not created from a text,
But through the practice of many, we overcome the test.
Love is an action verb in service it be true.
It gives and through giving creates the authority to rule.

Please believe the unbelievable and do what must be done.
To heal the unforgivable with love's brilliance, my son."

The Grandfather smiled at the students' applause.

"Thank you. It has been many years since I took that walk through the streets of Belfast. Fortunately, times have changed largely for the better. It is one of those interesting twists of fate that while we were in Belfast making an offering of our service, the unexpected did happen. International mediators and various leaders from each side negotiated agreements that helped usher in a period of peace.

"My hope is that this story will show how forgiveness can eventually break the negative cycle of

resentment and retaliation.

"In September of 1999, 35 volunteers from 15 nations gathered in Belfast as part of the RYS. The organizers publicly sought to recruit volunteers who were willing to work hard and invest in helping close the divide that separated different parts of the Belfast community. There was an unspoken awareness of the potential danger of coming to Belfast during this, the time of the troubles.

"The RYS challenge piqued the interest of an outstanding and diverse group of volunteers. Among those joining the team was Michael, a young African American minister from New Jersey, a Mongolian student, a Japanese Buddhist nun, and participants from India and Kenya, as well as the Seychelles, (an island off the coast of Africa).

"Many of us arrived in Belfast with mixed feelings. We held on to a romantic optimism about how dedicated people can contribute to positive change. Yet we were also worried about the potential mortal danger that our group could attract. Coming from diverse religious and cultural backgrounds, we soon came to an agreement that the shortest route to creating a bond of unity was to practice a spiritual insight found in every religion: selfless service.

"We worked and made decisions with an effort to keep the needs of others in the forefront. In doing this, each of us could grow in the awareness that life is too important to be simply just about 'me'. Yet, living an unselfish lifestyle requires much practice, and we were at best novices in need of a model to show and inspire us.

"Fortunately, we found that inspiration in the Columbanus Community.

The Columbanus Community in Belfast is a unique community staffed in large by religious people from the Roman Catholic and Protestant faiths. It is a model of Christian cooperation in a city crying out for healing and reconciliation. A palpable atmosphere of peaceful cooperation flowed through the community that was guided by a warm-hearted, New Zealand-born, Anglican clergywoman. The reverend and the community encouraged us to offer our service at the center, and we were happy to have that opportunity.

"The Columbanus Center serves the greater Belfast community in many ways. One quiet service it provides is a safe sanctuary for meetings between antagonists. Reconciliation work can be perilous in areas where people are murdered for trying. The center served to provide a protective cover for meetings of civic and political leaders, serving as a haven from the spotlight of media and the eyes of spies and snitches.

"Reconciliation and peace building require hard and often painstaking effort as relationships can be destroyed with one breach of faith or a misspoken word. At the time of our arrival, residents of Belfast had already reached a point where they were deeply searching for alternatives to violence. The Columbanus Community was playing a role in creating an environment for reconciliation and peace.

"Our team of volunteers were happy to work at the center and serve both the institution and the special people that worked there. The hosts requested that we clear a large, weedy field and transform it into a place that could be used for prayer, reflection, and relaxation. We responded, and over the next two weeks, our volunteers helped transform the area into a Peace Garden.

"At first, our enthusiasm was greeted by three days of heavy rain. The rain soaked the grounds we were clearing, and pools of water and mud formed. Soaking wet, digging soil, cutting trees, creating paths, step by step, we moved together. The rains provided us with a challenge that drew us into deeper communion. When the sun did arrive, we met it with hearts of appreciation and used its warmth as an excuse to linger in small, talkative groups. The sounds of our laughter and conversation were like a fresh musical score covering the edgy sounds of the larger Belfast community.

"In the twelve days allotted, we managed to shape the Peace Garden into something both attractive and practical. Set into the garden was a beautiful pagoda and a garden pool that was arched by a wooden bridge. The garden was anchored by a historic, stone Celtic Cross that had been built years before. The flowers and greenery added to the atmosphere, which was one where reflection and relaxation were natural.

"During our time working in the garden, many people were attracted by the lively activity. On our closing day, the Center hosted a special reconciliation ceremony led by local and international members of the Women's Federation for World Peace. The ceremony added to an already rich spiritual environment. Among the many attending the ceremony was an elderly gentleman, whom we will call Joseph. What happened to Joseph that day in the garden offers a clear sense of the impact labor of love can have.

"Joseph was rather short, with a slight tilt to him, a result of living some hard years on the planet. He carried the air of a person who had been more than willing to fight for what he thought was right. As a Roman Catholic in Belfast, he had spent his life hating those 'bloody English'. I imagine he had many a fight in his youthful glory days, but now he was approaching a time in life ripe for clearing one's heart and finding peace.

"Joseph entered the garden at the time of the reconciliation ceremony. He was visibly moved by the joy on people's faces and with the transformation of the field. Old Joseph asked who was responsible for creating the peace garden, and he was told that it was the young volunteers from different nations. He moved around, approached each young person, and offered his thanks.

"He would say to them; 'Well, lassie, what's your name, and where are you from?'

"The volunteer might answer back, 'I am Maria from Hungary.'

"Joseph would say, 'Oh, thank you, Maria. God bless you, and God bless Hungary.' He would then approach a young man and say, 'Laddie, what's your name, and where are you from?'

"The next person might say, 'I am Julio from Spain,' and Old Joe would bless him and then bless Spain.

"The happiness of Joseph and the happiness of all those in the garden seemed to be coming to a climax as Old Joe came closer and closer to William, who happened to be an English. People in the garden were aware of the potential disaster of seeing old antagonisms flare up on this supposed day of reconciliation.

"Old Joe approached William and said, 'Well, laddie, tell me, what's your name and where are you from?'

"'Well, sir, I am William, and I'm from England.'

" A silence followed. Joseph looked at William closely, giving him the up and down. He paused when his eyes came to grips with William's. After the eye-to-eye fix, we wondered what was going to happen.

"Then Joseph said, 'Well, William, God bless you, and God bless England!'

"At that magical moment, the garden's quiet ceased, human motion began, and laughter awkwardly jumped out as a way to ease hearts and minds. We had witnessed a miracle, not the walk-on-water type of miracle, but still an irrefutable miracle. Joseph could see William as the good young man he was, worthy of being blessed. If he was worthy of being blessed, then his country also must be worthy of blessing. William's heart and effort to build a garden allowed one man to liberate his heart from some of the pain of resentment.

"Real hurt and misunderstanding exist in our personal lives and in the lives of whole groups of people. When resentment is not resolved, it has the potential to generate anger that can lead to violence. Redirecting the resentment of those who have suffered is a critical challenge facing those who want to build peace. That was achieved in the Peace Garden through loving service to the community.

"Sincerity and hard work can often go a long way to facilitate the process of healing. Talk is cheap if it is not backed by action. In building the Peace Garden, we were actively contributing to the peace process one heart at a time. The president of Ireland, Mary Patricia McAleese, paid the Columbanus Center a visit and walked the garden paths. She was moved to come to Belfast to help the peace process as high-level international talks were underway. By her participation, she made a recognizable contribution to the process that was about to set a lasting peace in place.

"One may wonder why the president was drawn to the very spot where our team of global peacemakers had labored. Do these things simply happen by chance or do invisible forces guide them? It is hard to say what power is generated when committed people decide to offer their hearts, labor, and even risk their lives for a just cause. I can offer no analytic proof of positive changes that came from our efforts. It is a fact that after decades of unsuccessful negotiations, a successful peace initiative was put in place soon after our international volunteers made their offering.

"Was it simply an interesting twist of fate or were our efforts a contributing factor serving to tip the scale in favor of peace? What do you think?"

The answer was unanimous: the students, Mr. Bennet, and all the neighbors present were certain the efforts of the RYS had moved the peace process forward.

"I would be so devoutly grateful to believe so," said the Grandfather. "And may all your efforts contribute to peace as well."

Chapter 19: This Time the Japanese Are Invading with Love

"The heart has its reasons, which reason does not know."

Blaise Pascal

In the grassy knoll that served as a "stage" in the Grandfather's yard, Juan was playing his guitar. He was accompanied by Kyle on the keyboard and Chrissy on her violin. While the stout, huge Kyle and long, lanky Chrissy had contrasting body types, their music seemed to dance together in ways that only kindred spirits can. They read each other well and caught the nuances each used to invoke a song's message. They had to catch themselves at points and shift from the joy of making music together and riffing off on musical tangents. Juan was usually the one to call them back to the melody and main theme, gesturing with his guitar neck to indicate that they needed to pay attention to the task at hand: preparing the group of people gathered to receive the Grandfather's message.

The Grandfather had his eyes closed in a meditative mood. Juan gently ended the song with a sweet picking off a few strings, while Kyle wound down his thunder, and

Chrissy sounded one, last, shimmering note on her violin. Juan put down his guitar when he saw that the Grandfather was ready, his eyes open and bright, and the trio exchanged words of acknowledgement with each other. The three assumed seats in the front row as the Grandfather rose and noted his thanks.

"These three instrumentalists and songsters really bring magic to our meetings, don't they?" This brought a round of applause that startled and flattered Juan. He could see Chrissy and Kyle were also taken a little aback by it. "And you, my young friends, bring the sparkle and magic of your presence. To my neighbors, I am eternally thankful."

The adults from the neighborhood, who often stood in the back, shuffled their feet, smiled, and casted their eyes down modestly as all the young faces turned to them in appreciation.

"I'm sure you have found, even in your young lives, that there are sometimes barriers between people," began the Grandfather. "Just a few incidents may have built up where you started to question a person's motivation or truthfulness, and suddenly, you don't call or text one another as much anymore. Sometimes, there are quite large barriers between people who have had negative experiences with one another from the get-go. What do you think is the best path to overcome barriers?"

"Communication?" asked a girl in the second row.

"Ah, yes, communication," said the Grandfather. "In addition to skill in communication, it is also important to have the right heart behind what you communicate and to communicate it in ways people can understand. To me, as you know, one of the greatest means of communication is service. It says so much beyond words.

"I hope that today's story will show you one effective way to overcome barriers and shape a new future. The central characters of our story are a team of hard-working, young Japanese women and men who were kind, caring, and excited to offer their time and effort in a foreign land. They shared a desire to do something worthwhile and a willingness to learn from each other.

"Of equal importance to this story are the Mongolian young men and women who were part of the service project, as they believed and practiced the same things. Together they helped create an environment that would allow for transformation and healing rather than repeating the sorrows of history.

"In the summer of 1939, the Imperial Army of Japan attempted to aggressively expand its growing Asian empire, crossing the border of China and entering Mongolia with tanks, airplanes, and thousands of soldiers. The Japanese fought hard and paid the price in blood, while the Mongolians lost civilians and soldiers alike in the effort to defend their country. Eventually, Mongolian soldiers, with the assistance of troops and logistical support from the Soviet Union, drove the invaders back across the border.

"Sixty years later, in the late days of the truly short Mongolian summer, 30 volunteers from Japan, Mongolia, China, Malaysia, Korea, Singapore, and the USA participated in an RYS project that was designed to promote cooperation across national, cultural, and religious differences. Mongolia was selected as the host nation because it was going through a challenging period of transition following the collapse of its ally, the Soviet Union. Our multinational team of volunteers had made a choice to offer service and to make new friends.

"Mongolia is a land of broad, sweeping plains and crisp blue skies. Standing on the plains, one can understand how its ancient horsemen, masters of archery, chose to ride out toward the distant horizon and find new lands. This urge for discovery eventually made them heirs to one of the largest empires in the world.

"In contrast, the cramped capital city of Ulan Bator is stripped of much of its natural beauty. On first arriving, one is struck by the multitudes of tall, dull apartment buildings constructed especially to provide shelter from the stark, long winters. Beauty was not part of the Soviet-influenced architectural plan.

"While staying in the capital, our group enjoyed trips into the neighboring countryside where we could hike and ford the smaller rivers, using ropes to keep us from being swept away by the currents. Most of our daylight hours were spent working either at a Buddhist temple or at an elementary school where we were creating a playground. During our second week in the capital, our schedule offered free time during which we could participate in a variety of optional activities.

"Several Mongolian ladies jumped on this

opportunity since they longed to show their Japanese

Work at the school

friends, Haruko, Hiromi, Setsuko, Yoko, and Yumie, parts

of the capital that they loved. The Japanese ladies were

excited to have the chance to see more of Ulan Bator and

incredibly happy that they were doing this with their

Mongolian friends. I was able to join this group and

crammed myself into the van along with the others.

"Despite linguistic struggles—the type that would

usually hinder communication—the Mongolian and

Japanese ladies seemed to have a special connection and

really enjoyed each other's company. Laughter punctuated

our lively sharing as we drove to historic sites as well as to some of the girls' favorite locations. The five Japanese women were effervescently happy since they had made this long journey to Mongolia, not only hoping that their service would provide something good for children and their families but also because they really wanted to make new friends.

"In an effort to pull me into their experience, Yumie shared something that everyone in the van felt: 'We just get along so well with all the volunteers, and our friendship seems to grow each day we work together painting the Buddhist temple. What we are doing at the temple and the school speaks to the reasons why we are here.'

"Later that afternoon, our van twisted its way up a hill to a place where we sighted a large stone monument. The formidable statue stood with dignity near the ledge of a hill that overlooked the city. People were walking up the steep hill to go to the area where the monument stood. Haruko asked if we could please stop the van to see the monument and enjoy the panoramic view.

"The driver pulled the van to a halt, and we piled out and made the walk up the hill. We walked up a pathway accompanied by families and small groups who seemed to be on a kind of pilgrimage. As we approached the statue, we could see a series of large stone walls etched with names and written accounts of the defense of the capital. The monument site commemorated the Mongolian and Soviet resistance to the Japanese invaders. This week marked the 60th anniversary of the Japanese invasion of Mongolia.

"None of us had been aware of this anniversary, and the timing added an emotional poignancy to our visit. Like most Japanese youth, the volunteers knew little about Japan's role in World War II. When the girls realized what Japan had done in Mongolia, a country that they were growing to love, they were shocked. Some began to weep; all had tears in their eyes. The shame of history weighed heavily on each of them.

"After some time had passed, the young Japanese volunteers turned desperately to their Mongolian friends and repeatedly said, 'We are so sorry, so sorry. We did not know this happened, and we are so sorry. Can you forgive us?'

"Their Mongolian friends looked surprised at their request. 'My friends,' they said, 'the Japanese came 60 years ago with tanks and soldiers to conquer. You come with love and service to paint our temples and fix our schools. You are Japan to us. You have made a new and special relationship with our country and with us. We love Japan because of you.'

"There is a simple beauty to this Mongolian experience shared between the grandchildren of former enemies. Young Japanese and Mongolians are the central characters, but it could be repeated with people from other backgrounds. The constants in this formula for healing are the elements of sacrifice and loving service.

"This story stands in stark contrast to the news stories we too often read. Media accounts often harm our hearts as they retell stories of hatred and brutality performed by those who fail to forgive, who fail to reach out and make peace with themselves and with others. As long as people are full of resentment, there is no room for love.

"Resentment has a monstrous power if it is let loose to seek its own course. The spirit of resentment seems to have a life of its own. It is not resolved, and it does not disappear without being properly addressed.

"Resentment, like love, is invisible. Both are real; both can and do affect the world. Love can be generated when things are rightly ordered, when giving and receiving run their natural course as water flowing in a river. Love is the central axis of the original plan of creation.

"Both love and resentment are moved by reasons that are beyond reason—as the French philosopher Blaise Pascal once counselled, 'The heart has its reasons, which reason does not know.' Behind both love and resentment are powerful spiritual forces. Each is capable of digesting the other. When resentment swallows love, the results are always destructive. When love swallows resentment, it produces a great transformation for the good. Of the two, love and resentment, only one will last through eternity. Our Mongolian friends chose love. Let us all choose love."

The grandfather nodded to Juan, and he and Chrissy and Kyle jumped up to play a finale. It was a sing-along, familiar to all the students, and it was accompanied by hand-clapping as well.

As the Grandfather participated in the singing and clapped his hands, even occasionally hopping from one foot to another while the students cheered, Juan smiled with satisfaction. The Grandfather was fully back and better than ever.

Chapter 20: Walking the Path of a Peacemaker

"The greatest friend of truth is Time, her greatest enemy is Prejudice, and her constant companion is Humility."
Charles Caleb Colton

Juan couldn't believe it! He'd had a fight with Chrissy. And over a song! Or was it really over a song?

Usually, they were so agreeable. Was he jealous, he wondered, of how well Kyle and Chrissy clicked musically? Was he tired of having to be the grounded one, the one with his eye on the end rather than the means? Was he shouldering too much, trying to set the tone for every class and story? Did he think Chrissy liked Kyle more than she liked him? What was it?

All he knew was that, when the three of them were speculating over lunch about the music for the next day's class at the Grandfather's, he had suddenly blown up at Chrissy and stalked away. He'd glanced back and had seen Kyle shrug and tuck into his lunch with vigor while Chrissy sat back, looking completely stunned. Then he saw Chrissy tap Kyle on the arm in exasperation and say something like,

'How can you eat a time like this, you big oaf?" to which Kyle shrugged. All that, somehow, made him feel a little better.

Juan couldn't even remember exactly what he'd said to her in his explosion. It was something like, "You act like you are the big boss of everything here, and like you know it all, and are on top of everything, and like I don't know what I'm doing. Are you really so much better than everyone else?"

He supposed he should apologize, but he didn't want to. Sometimes Chrissy acted like she alone understood the Grandfather, his heart, and his messages, and she alone had the talent and expertise to bring that across to their audience through music.

Fine. She could do it all herself then. She and Kyle!

He ignored her in the classes they shared, but he was also conscious that time was ticking by and that they had better agree on a song before the following afternoon.

That night he got a text from Kyle: "Chrissy is going to do a solo tomorrow. She thinks you and I need some rest."

That was diplomatic. At least she wasn't going to perform just with Kyle, leaving him out and maybe raising questions in people's minds. Still, he knew Kyle didn't need any "rest". Kyle had the energy to spare—too much of it, most of the time.

He didn't ask to go early to the Grandfather's, and Mr. Bennet, glancing between him and Chrissy, didn't press him to do so. He sauntered there with the rest of the class, deliberately not walking near Chrissy or Kyle. He took place in the third row, just like a regular member of the class instead of the music leader.

Chrissy got up. She wet her lips nervously, obviously trying not to look at Juan. She announced that she had written the song she was going to sing herself.

In addition to her violin expertise, Juan had heard that Chrissy was a very capable music maker with a guitar, and she brought up a guitar for this solo number. Yeah, she was good. Juan could tell that from the opening bars. The girl did have musical talent. He looked down at the ground and listened to the words of the song she had written.

Chrissy sang, hesitantly at first, about "Being on the Top of the Heap." It was a song about appearances and how sometimes someone seemed strong and on top of things and like they had all the answers. The truth was, though, that person might be just as afraid and vulnerable as everyone else and sometimes acted tough out of insecurity.

Juan could tell that every student could identify with the song. There was a deep, contemplative silence as Chrissy finished, quietly put down her guitar, and assumed a seat with her head bowed. The applause, though subdued, was heartfelt. Juan saw some of the girls touching Chrissy's arm to get her attention and thank her for the song and her honesty.

The Grandfather walked slowly to the central position on the grass.

"Thank you, Chrissy," he said. "Sometimes, it is not easy to tell what another person is thinking inside until they speak out about who they really are. That's especially true if the person or group they represent seems to be 'on the top of the heap', as you put it. That relates very well to our story today."

As the Grandfather began to speak, Juan found it hard to listen. He was thinking about Chrissy's song. He wondered if it was a kind of musical apology. After all,

Chrissy had been really bossy lately, acting like she had it all together. He glanced at her, and she saw him look at her, but she looked down and away.

"I am going to introduce a dear friend of mine, David Earle, through the story," the Grandfather said. "Today, we will talk about how David did his part in helping to heal a wound in the hearts of people in India, some of whom had known the English as colonial masters who treated Indians as if they were an inferior people, in need of English guidance. Perhaps you know that Mohandas K. Gandhi led the Indian people to independence from the British empire. He did it through non-violence and through refusing to attack or hate the British, in spite of their history as oppressors. Eventually, he helped them to realize that they shouldn't be trying to manage India and that their ways were not necessarily the right ones for India. The British withdrew, many of them with respect and genuine regard for Gandhi.

"At a future gathering, we will look at how Dr. David took his initial experience in India and brought it back to his home in Birmingham, England. In fact, he returned to India to help create an interreligious orphanage.

His work stimulated the government of India to award him honorary Indian citizenship.

"Let us start with some words from Charles Caleb Colton, as they help set up our story: 'The greatest friend of truth is Time, her greatest enemy is Prejudice, and her constant companion is Humility.' I think David's humility is a major feature of this story.

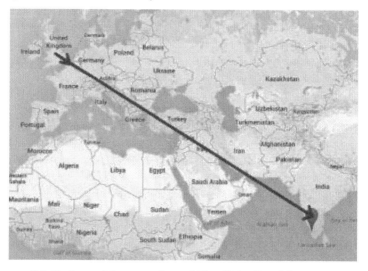

"Tall, lean, blue-eyed, and English, David was not afraid of hard work or creative approaches to deal with problems. He invested himself into earning his Ph.D., but he never let that achievement put a distance between himself and others. David possessed a gift for being able to recognize the value in each person regardless of race, religion, or background. He used his gifts to better his life and the lives of those around him.

"Living in the multicultural city of Birmingham, David and his wife Patricia attended a variety of interreligious programs, where their concern for religious cooperation was reciprocated. The programs they attended often attracted a wide assortment of religious devotees, many of whom had roots in India. It was during this time that Marshal D'Souza, the national director of the RYS, heard of David's interest in interreligious service work. Marshal called David and suggested he should join an upcoming project in Kerala, India. For David, the upcoming project and its venue in India were especially appealing.

"Aware of the British colonial legacy and the impact it had made in India, he approached his trip with a strong desire to serve the Indian people. Often in the past, British adventurers, traders, merchants, and soldiers went to India for purposes other than benevolent giving. David was driven by a motivation to contribute to building a different type of legacy.

"David made the journey from England to the rural village of Karukutty. In the village, he was met by 100 RYS volunteers representing seven religions and nine nations.

"The village of Karukutty had narrow dirt roads that were strained by a heavy increase in various forms of vehicles. Encouraged by the local community, the central focus of our work was widening the roads.

"Workdays began early, providing a way for us to catch the cooler morning air. With picks, shovels, and buckets in hand, we formed long lines down the street and began our digging. Before long, villagers from neighboring houses would step up with some tools and join in the shoveling and the transport of large roadside stones.

This RYS project was truly fortunate to have as a partner Gramswaraj, a rural development organization running in cooperation with Mahatma Gandhi University. They sent teams of students to villages where they lived, worked, and gained practical field experience in their areas of study.

"Gramswaraj's efforts were designed to apply Gandhian principles in sustainability and development to practical village life. Our RYS team members worked side by side with the student practitioners and gained insights into the local culture as well as practical insights into the teachings of Mahatma Gandhi.

"In the evenings, both the international participants and those from different parts of India took time to share song and dance. David, guitar in hand, was among the performers. When the news of our multicultural entertainment traveled, we found ourselves receiving numerous invitations to bring the group to neighboring villages.

"Following a day of work, on several consecutive evenings, we were welcomed by large, curious audiences in various villages. During our time together, we shared our songs and, in return, enjoyed the local children and young people's offerings of traditional songs and dances. The village staging areas for these events were quite simple. Often the curtain and backdrop were tattered with holes. Yet, in these modest settings, we found ourselves immersed in the rich cultural heritage of rural India.

"Despite being older than most of the volunteers, David wasted no time jumping into the project. Some of the older villagers looked at David with a special curiosity. David was friendly and worked hard, but historic memories of other Englishmen in India managed to stir up a certain skepticism. It is not difficult to imagine one villager whispering to another, 'You can never really know what those English are up to, can you?' Suspicion of David was in the air.

"After laboring for several hours on the second workday, we were ready to take our scheduled break. Snacks brought by neighbors were set aside in an area where some were waiting to serve us. David looked up at the gathering crowd, grabbed his shovel, and approached.

"He called out in a strong voice, with dirt on his hands and sweat dripping down his face. He raised his shovel high and proclaimed, 'My friends, today the British have returned to India, but this time with shovel-in-hand to help you build your roads!'

"Then David beamed a disarming smile at those gathered from the neighborhood. A note of genuine surprise could be read on their faces. David's zeal, along with his spirit of humility, was well-received. Soon, community members drew near to David and, with smiles, offered him snacks, drinks, and friendly conversation. There was now room in everyone's heart as David took to eating his snack, sharing and listening as if in the company of lifelong family and friends.

"In the days and weeks ahead, we continued to share our food, conversations, and laughter with those living in the village. It was clear to many of us that the invisible barriers that had divided us were gone. Replacing the divide was a new sense of warmth and friendship.

"In an almost mystical way, some observers commented that the barriers seemed to come down when a hard-working Englishman proclaimed, 'My friends, the

English have returned to India, but this time with shovel-in-hand to help you build your roads.'

"Resentment is an invisible force that can accumulate, layer upon layer, throughout the course of time. The history of people mistreating, abusing, and taking advantage of each other adds to the weight of resentment. Resentment is often an unwanted legacy, one that is passed on from generation to generation until something is done to reverse it.

"Overcoming resentment is indispensable for our personal health and happiness, and it is an essential ingredient of peace. While we cannot go back into history and heal past injustices, we can offer acts of human kindness that serve as an invitation to replace anger and resentment with a more powerful force—the force of love. Unselfish service touches people's hearts and in the process moves the very heart of God."

The students applauded the Grandfather, and then there was a moment of confusion. Juan, Chrissy, and Kyle usually offered some sort of musical number as a closing. Juan kept his head down, waiting for Chrissy to take the lead, as it seemed to him she so obviously wanted to do.

Someone nudged him. He looked up, and there was Chrissy, offering her guitar to him.

"You can borrow my shovel," she said softly.

He took Chrissy's guitar. It was a nice one and only took a second to nestle into his hands and offer its strings invitingly to him. He played a song he had been practicing secretly and was rewarded with a strong round of applause when he was finished.

When he handed the guitar back to Chrissy, she smiled and said humbly, "Great job. You are one heck of a musician. We're all in this working together, aren't we?"

"Yeah," he said.

"Sorry if I forgot that."

"Apology accepted."

Juan felt his heart and the quarrel healed as he headed over to the refreshment table for some treats before everything was put away—or before Kyle, who was there first, consuming everything in sight.

Chapter 21: A Dream Deferred but Not Forever

What happens to a dream deferred?

Does it dry up

Like a raisin in the sun?

Or fester like a sore--

And then run?

Does it stink like rotten meat?

Or crust and sugar over--

like a syrupy sweet?

Maybe it just sags

like a heavy load.

Or does it explode?

Langston Hughes

The Grandfather asked one of the students, Pete, to read Langston Hughes's poem, a "Dream Deferred", in front of the gathered class at the next meeting. When Pete had read it out loud with good diction and projection, the Grandfather nodded in satisfaction.

The Grandfather began.

"I'm going to tell you about a dream deferred, put off for twenty-one years: a dream that seemed impossible at times. This dream nevertheless came true. One of the reasons it came true was because it did not explode, as the last line of the poem says. There was little to no violence in the aptly named 'Velvet Revolution' that took place in Czechoslovakia in 1989. Yet freedom was victorious through the sheer power of the will of the people. It was really a miracle.

"Have you ever wondered about the shelf life of resentment? Does it have an expiration date? How long do deep resentments last? Do they end after the passing of a few seasons or continue till the end of our living memory? Are they capable of being passed down over generations, shaping a painful legacy? Do resentments linger and grow stronger over time, or can they simply fade away?

"We all have hurt others during our lives; each of us at some time has had to consider how or if we can restore a damaged relationship. Perhaps after having a major disagreement, did you consider ways, methods, and actions that could move your relationship and the healing process forward?

"I have seen how some former political prisoners, unjustly incarcerated, forgave their captors. They found ways to let go of the resentment in their hearts and move on to enjoy rich and rewarding lives. In contrast, I met those who were stuck in the past and could not move beyond past injustices or focus their energy on building a brighter future.

"In 1991, I traveled to Czechoslovakia, a nation that had been one of the most repressive of the Soviet satellites in Eastern Europe. It had recently undergone a non-violent revolution led by an astute playwright, Vaclav Havel. The wave of new religious, political, and economic freedoms was just starting to become a way of life for ordinary citizens.

"Before this non-violent, 'Velvet Revolution', the Communist Party had ruled the nation for 40 years under the strong arm and sharp eyes of the Soviet Union. The government controlled all aspects of life, including artistic and religious expression. It was tough on those that did not conform, especially those active in church work. Control was something the Communist government was reluctant to cede to any other master and certainly not to God.

"The liberation in 1989 was a triumph of the human spirit. The citizens of Prague had suffered much over the previous fifty years. A brutal, six-year Nazi occupation and subjugation had taken place in 1939. During that bitter time, the rulers systematically sent trainloads of families to concentration camps where Jews, gypsies, homosexuals, and others were heartlessly worked to death or systematically murdered.

"After the collapse of Nazi Germany, freedom was short-lived. Soon new masters, the Communist Party, seized control of various levels of government. The government turned into an 'all seeing, all controlling' military state under the watchful eyes of the Soviet Union.

"There was a time in 1968 when things seemed to be changing for the better in Czechoslovakia. It was optimistically called the Prague Spring. Reforms were loosening some of the stifling government restrictions. The thaw energized idealistic university students. My friends were among those who spoke out publicly, sharing their hopes for freedom as well as spiritual insights. As the size of the spiritual and religious gatherings grew, they attracted closer scrutiny from the eyes of the nearly omniscient security forces. A hideous crackdown followed. The government threw those who were speaking out into prison.

"Among my friends, one young church leader died in prison, her body eventually broken down from the beating, cold, hunger, and medical indifference. Most of my church's core group spent over a year in prison, a fate shared by other active religious groups.

"My friend Juri spent more than a year in a dank, dark, miserable prison in the prime of life for the 'crime' of believing in God and sharing a message of inspiration.

"I became friends with Juri in the months following the Velvet Revolution. We teamed up on the work to create a multi-religious, international service project. The project was something that would have seemed an impossible dream only a few years before. However, with sincere effort, we were able to create a three-week project. When the launch time arrived, 110 volunteers from 16 nations and each major religion found ways to contribute to its success.

"Juri was able to shape work activities that were aimed at helping individuals and communities through tree planting, light construction work, and cultural exchanges. Throughout our time together, we worked, slept, ate, played sports and games, exchanged cultural insights, discussed issues, and freely shared our often-differing ideas and beliefs.

"For Juri, it was an amazing reversal of the dark days he had known as a college student. The rediscovered freedoms of this new age helped stimulate Juri and many others as they moved to inaugurate a period of creativity, imagination, and hope throughout society.

"Juri was able to maintain a positive outlook on life even though it took 21 years for the hopes of the Prague Spring to be actualized. Having his hopes so long deferred could have crushed his spirit and shaped him into a cynic. Instead, when we met, he looked much younger than his age, and his eyes lit with a consistent twinkle. He was delighted in his role as a parent as he and his wife raised six beautiful and energetic children. He could smile, knowing that those children would live in a much better environment than their parents had.

"I cannot help but wonder, what would I do if thrown in prison on account of my beliefs? If I were thrown into prison for doing God's work, well, I might ask God a few serious questions behind those prison walls: questions like, 'Why me'? Or 'Is this is what I get for listening to You?' Hopefully, I would find the faith and courage to respond as Juri did.

"Juri, an innocent and good man, reacted to his unjust punishment with quiet courage. It is amazing to me how he and so many others who suffered during those times managed to forgive their oppressors and move their lives forward. Still, others did not. Those are, I think, the real victims of all the oppression.

"It was at this time of new hope in 1989 that I accepted an invitation to attend a youth meeting at a Protestant church in Prague. I expected to meet with young, forward-looking leaders eager to shape the future. Some leaders were like that. Unfortunately, there were also some congregants that were held captive by a spirit of resentment. It was the kind of resentment that blocked their ability to see or seek a path towards resolution and reconciliation. Some were full of resentment towards the recent Communist government; some were angry at what the Nazis had done a generation before. But it was Jakob's resentments that struck me the most, for he held on to historic memories of religious conflict originating long centuries past.

"Jakob, a church youth leader, spoke with an immediacy and passion that was inflamed by injustices committed eons ago. The injustices that happened in his and his parents' lifetime did not appear to be of the same deep concern to him. He was obsessed with injustices that his co-religionists had suffered four centuries before, when Europe was going through the bloody pains of religious upheaval and war. To some contemporaries, those events would be considered informative footnotes of history, but to him, they were alive with relevance. Listening to Jakob, I caught a deep insight into the nature of lingering resentment. Passionate Jakob was driven to explain, 'They (the Catholics) made our ministers galley slaves; can you imagine that! They were sent to the Mediterranean Sea, bound in chains, and worked to death. Such things happened not only to ministers as whole families were put to the sword: innocent believers, those that refused to give up their faith. How could those Catholics claim to be Christians?'

"Jakob's words rang with such emotion, it was as if he was sharing from yesterday's headlines. I wondered why the wounds of the past were still festering in him. Why, as a young man, wasn't he thinking of investing his energy into creating a better future? I began to realize resentment can take on a life of its own. We all need to take resentment seriously, as it affects things as important as marriage, race relations, war, and peace.

"Jacob's resentments originated over four hundred years ago, and they still needed resolution. Resentment can be passed on from one generation to the next. How many grandmothers shared these and other sad stories with their grandchildren, and how many fathers encouraged their sons to grow strong so that they could avenge the past? Until a true reconciliation occurs, the often-invisible element of resentment will find ways to reappear.

"While governments can help facilitate the healing process, their powers are relatively limited. It is essentially the task of men and women of goodwill to model a path of loving one's enemies and forgiving the unforgivable. No government can effectively legislate this—it is the common task of all of us.

"People of faith may be better equipped with insights and examples that encourage us to forgive. Jesus as a master teacher pleaded, 'Father forgive them for they know not what they do.' The quality of his love and the quality of our love can help us, individually and collectively, be released from the burdens of resentment. Such liberation can help us as parents, as children, as family members, and as friends.

"I wish for you the power of a love that heals, a love that makes two into one, a love that hopes, and a love that serves. Find joy in your days and spread joy in your lives. Let us be the healers that can embody the simple principle of living for the sake of others through service."

On the way back to school, Chrissy and Juan drifted, quite naturally, into walking side by side.

"Why did you call your guitar a shovel?" he asked her.

Chrissy shrugged. "I guess I wanted you to know that, even if I was being too bossy, I was working hard too. We were all digging that road together."

"Oh. Nice shovel."

"Thanks."

Juan looked rather shame-facedly at Chrissy. Although he had accepted her apology, he had had a hard time completely letting go of his resentment over her "take charge" ways. Yet, if the Grandfather's friend Juri could forgive those who had imprisoned him and have enough hope to build a new future after 21 years of waiting—well, he guessed he could forgive Chrissy and be friends with her once again.

Chrissy began to hum a tune, Juan joined in, and pretty soon, the whole group was singing a familiar song as they headed back to their school.

Chapter 22: "You Treated Us as Sisters"

"Resentment is like drinking poison and then hoping it will kill your enemies."

Nelson Mandela

Mr. Bennet rapped his knuckles on his desk to bring the chattering class to attention.

"I've got an announcement to make, class. Most of your families received an email about the change of schedule today, but I'll reiterate the message here. The rest of the school is being let out a half hour early today for a principals' conference. So, I would like you to bring with you to the Grandfather's for any books or equipment you need to take home, as, by the time we get back to the school, it will be closed. Yes, you will have to carry your things to the Grandfather's, but there is a reward: you can go home straight from there according to your parents' arrangements, or you can stay longer there too, if you have your parents' permission to do so. I believe some of the neighbors mentioned a dinner party, or something like that."

The class broke into cheers.

"We'll skip the musical or other introduction, and the Grandfather will plunge right into his story so that you won't be kept longer 'in school' than any of the other students. You'll be free right after the story ends."

Juan fretted all the way to the Grandfather's. For one thing, he was carrying more than he was used to (although he'd never complained about carrying his guitar there). He'd been kept off the stage for two weeks now. Yes, he'd had a tiff with Chrissy, but why couldn't he play and sing this week? Was Mr. Bennet really trying to save time, or was he, Juan, being punished for having an argument?

It didn't seem fair. After all, the quarrel had been Chrissy's fault. She shouldn't have been so bossy.

The Grandfather was waiting on "the story green" on his lawn. After greeting them with outstretched arms, inviting them all to stay as long as they wanted to after the story, he went right into his tale.

"The story that I will share takes place at a time when the world was anxiously watching South Africa. The system of apartheid had officially ended with an elected change of government. No longer would people be racially classified and segregated. There was great hope for improvement in people's daily lives, especially those who had faced the heaviest limitations during the apartheid era.

"Unanswered questions remained. Would people who enjoyed the privileges of ruling allow that special status to pass peacefully? Would those that suffered under the oppression of apartheid take the moral high ground and offer a path for reconciliation to the former rulers? Or would resentment rule the day?

"In 1998, two strong cultural currents were pushing for changes in the 'new' South Africa. One current, encouraged by religious sentiment, understood the power of grace, forgiveness, and love. A second current, fueled by unresolved resentments and Marxist ideology, sought to even the scales through retribution and punishment. Which way would the nation go?

"If you search Marx for words concerning love, mercy, forgiveness, and reconciliation, you will not find them. The cry for justice is important to the Marxist, but can justice take root without forgiveness and love? Can we imagine such an outcome? If this ideology governed South Africa, it would demand satisfaction that would inevitably lead to the shedding of much blood.

"South Africa is a multi-religious nation with large segments of its people being Christian, Hindu, and Muslim, while others practice traditional African beliefs. Adherents of each religion tended to cluster together and take care of their own with little or no cooperation with each other. The peaceful transition in South Africa would require cooperation that was beyond the structures of religious dogma. The deep values and norms of each religion needed to find new ways of expression in an integrated and multi-religious society.

"The religious currents of that time were crying out, 'We are all children of God', but the Marxist worldview classified people as being either oppressors or the oppressed, a revolutionary or a reactionary. Reconciliation appeared impossible.

"Fortunately, the newly elected President, Nelson Mandela, carried with him a hard-earned moral authority that he used to widen a path to peaceful reconciliation. The Truth and Reconciliation Commission, set up by the Mandela government, provided an environment for repentance, forgiveness, and reconciliation.

"Marxist materialism fails to account for the spiritual side of life. The Truth and Reconciliation Commission dug deeper and found a way to speak respectfully and listen to people's hearts and minds. President Mandela and the members of the commission were able to provide a more holistic response to the challenges of South Africa at that time in its history. For this, we owe a debt of thanks.

"Soweto is an area where some of the most damaging and lethal riotings took place during the last stages of the apartheid era in South Africa. On my first visit to South Africa, my working partner, Massimo Trombin, and I did a seminar in Soweto. There we saw the first-hand difficult living conditions that existed. We met with residents in this overcrowded area and listened and asked questions.

"Soweto's chaotic streets captured little of the natural beauty that is such a part of this country. Most residents had little or no experience visiting the beautiful parts of South Africa and had no experience with its diverse wildlife. Few realized what they were missing or what spending time in nature's beauty could do for one's state of mind. From this visit, we were able to sense that a service project held in a national park could provide a unique opportunity for discovery and sharing.

"Our South African friends, Brigetta Wakabashi and Bushy Rankale were invested in making project preparations. They selected beautiful Gauteng National Park for our site, where we would live and work on an environmental project with the cooperation and guidance of park rangers. Short on funding, Brigetta, Bush, and I went to local grocery stores and asked that they help provide food donations for the project. We were well received, and many gave generously. Business owners and store managers opened their hearts and pantries on hearing our plan.

"On the morning of the project, we met at a central location for a short orientation. The work projects at the park were designed by the park workers keenly aware of the necessary ecological balance. As part of the preparations, participants and staff were asked to consider what our shared spiritual responsibility was to the environment. We arranged to discuss our thoughts by a campfire under a multitude of stars. The fresh air, clear night sky, and crisp temperatures helped to keep our sharing lively.

"We slept in simple cabins near dry, green hills and were greeted in the morning by families of baboons. Most of the participants had never seen baboons living in the wild, and they were excited. Really excited! The beauty of nature just hours away from their home was totally unfamiliar to them, and it was full of fresh discoveries.

"In our group, we had two young black South Africans who were members of a Hindu sect devoted to Krishna. The two had clearly changed their lifestyles in the pursuit of a life of deeper meaning. Their commitment served to stimulate the participants from the other traditions. No longer was the street talk of the city acceptable in conversation in our mixed company. By speaking and acting respectfully, the Hindu devotees' comportment offered a silent challenge to the pride of some of the Christian men. A mild positive competition arose on who would provide the best models of service and equanimity.

"The young women in our group noticed the difference in the ways the men were relating to them. The mean streets were as far away as the macho male hunter attitude they had known. Males no longer strutted with aggressive boldness or shot predatory glares at the ladies.

Replacing it was a more familiar tone, marked by warmth and courtesy.

"On our final night together, we were gathered around our campfire and offered our reflections of the time together. We shared our work and our various experiences. We sang and sang, and some danced.

"At one point, a young lady rose in the circle and looked at the men.

"'I want to say something to the men in this circle,' she said. 'Please try to understand the meaning and gratitude that I will try to express. I want to thank all the men for treating us like your sisters. We women had such a good experience during this time. We had a wonderful sense of freedom because we could act like a family and not be worried. Thank you.'

"It was a simple declaration of appreciation from this woman, yet it meant so much.

"Where do we learn how to respect and love someone of the opposite sex? It is in the family. Many of those in the circle had received the nourishment of love from a brother or sister, but others were nearly starving from a lack of that kind of love. The RYS experience managed to melt us all into one unique family. In this family, we could grow to trust, love, and respect each other. This is an important step in creating an environment for lasting peace, and I was grateful to be a part of it.

"There is no better starting place than the family to start learning the lessons of love and life. The support unit of the family is really a gift from God. In a genuine sense, the family is the school of love, and love is what we should value most in life.

The family is a training ground where we go through a wide variety of difficulties and challenges. We learn to share, to compromise, to support, to receive unconditional love while contributing to something larger than ourselves. Families bear pain together, and though they also inflict hurt on each other, it is within the framework of the family that they find solace and forgiveness with a resilience that defies logic.

"Since boys and girls often see and experience things in different ways, siblings of the opposite sex can develop insights into the nature of their future spouse by observing, listening, and sharing.

"I realize most of us have had far from a perfect family life. The family falls short of being the perfect school of love, but listen with your heart to the cries of street children, see the lonely tears of forgotten senior citizens, feel the anguish of the suicidal teenager, and realize that all could use the support of a loving family.

"The family is a powerful miracle, and it is a model for the kind of beautiful love that can be expressed when we treat others as brothers and sisters."

The smells of the foods the neighbors had been quietly bringing out to put on the tables were becoming overpowering. The students, especially the boys, had their heads up, sniffing the air.

Mr. Bennet dismissed the class, and they began to pile on the tables. Juan was as hungry as any of them, and he moved to fill a plate as rapidly as he could. Then he saw several girls he didn't know well standing apart, looking overpowered by the guys. Chrissy was among them.

"Hey, guys," he said. "Let's give the girls a chance. I'll bet they're hungry too."

Fortunately, Kyle backed him up. Kyle was huge, and no one ever knew what he was going to do.

"Yeah," Kyle said in a gruff voice. "Ladies first, you guys!"

Juan handed Chrissy an empty plate.

"You go before me," he said.

"Thank you, Juan," she said with that new humility, and he felt like an arrow of truth went into his heart. In their quarrel, Chrissy had been wrong, but so had he. He wondered how many times he had overridden her, just like the guys were overriding the girls around the table. Maybe she had gotten bossy in self-defense.

"Would you like to sit together?" she invited him and Kyle.

She certainly could be nice, Juan thought.

"I would love to sit together," he said.

Kyle said, "Wherever. Whatever. I just want to eat."

Juan and Chrissy shared an understanding smile.

"Maybe we could start to plan the music for the next class," Chrissy suggested, a little tentatively.

"I would love to plan the music for the next class," said Juan. "I miss planning with you, and I miss performing with you."

Chrissy's smile was a radiant beam.

Soon, some parents began arriving to pick up their children from the early school release. The Grandfather and his neighbors invited them to participate in the feast. Some had to be convinced to put aside their busy schedules to spend time at this unusual gathering, but many did. The picnic became a family affair, and the Grandfather looked like he was in his element.

Part V: The Wonderful Power of One

Chapter 23: You Are Needed

"I slept and dreamt that life was joy. I awoke and saw that life was service. I acted and behold, service was joy."

Rabindranath Tagore

Mr. Bennet thought the students would be excited to begin planning a service project of their own. He was wrong.

It wasn't that they lacked ideas or that there was a dearth need in their community. Instead, the students seemed to lack confidence. Few of them believed they could serve or make any difference. They said things like:

"I'm too busy trying to solve my own problems."

"I'm too shy to approach people in the community."

"I'm too young to understand what the adults in my community face."

"I'm too out of shape to serve. I couldn't keep up with the work."

Mr. Bennet visited the Grandfather after a stymied planning session in school and vented to him about the students' defeatist attitudes.

"Everybody's 'too' something to do a service project!" Mr. Bennet complained, sipping Turkish coffee in the Grandfather's colorful living room. "I can't get them out of their chairs!"

"Well," said the Grandfather. "They have some sessions left with me. Maybe I can boost their confidence a little."

Although Chrissy, Juan, and Kyle began the next session with inspiring music about moving mountains, scaling peaks, and soaring high, the Grandfather could see that the musicians' hearts were not in it. The class was having a crisis of confidence, all right.

"Good afternoon, everyone," he greeted them. "Let me begin by saying that most of the truly great leaders of service I have met were quite ordinary people. Oh, if you search, you may possibly find a defender of peace in a leadership position but, more likely, they appear as ordinary citizens. These ordinary citizens simply want to improve the lives of those around them. They are the real champions.

"I'd like to tell you about one RYS volunteer who almost became an RYS reject! He was too old for the program. The program involved a lot of physical work, so we had an age limit of 30. Father Nithiya Sagayam was past 30, so, by the rules, he was just too old.

"Now, rules exist for a reason, and those reasons are often important. Yet, in some ways, Fr. Nithiya's clear and pure motivation spoke louder than the rules. We decided to make an exception for Fr. Nithiya, and I am glad we did.

"Fr. Nithiya arrived in Hungary for a month-long RYS project during the summer of 1991. The nation was bursting with decades of pent-up energy. Communism was out, and capitalism was coming in. There was suddenly free-market competition in goods, services, and ideas. Creativity was blooming, and international music, culture, and entertainment were pouring in.

"Nearly 100 volunteers and staff from 40 nations arrived in Budapest for orientation. This initial contact offered a chance to mix and socialize with peers from all over the world. During the orientation, we participated in various team-building exercises and enjoyed visits to the city's rich historic and cultural areas. At the conclusion of the orientation, we divided into three teams and traveled to separate areas where we would live and work on a variety of projects.

"Fr. Nithiya and his team went by bus to the industrial city of Tatabanya, where they were warmly welcomed by the residents. While in Tatabanya, our volunteers and staff slept in a dormitory at night, and during the day, we worked on repairing and expanding four community schools. Despite these schools being closed for summer break, we were often visited by young students anxious to meet us.

"Many in Tatabanya had never seen an African, a Malaysian, or a South American. For the locals observing our diverse international group, it must have seemed remarkable that we could communicate freely, share lighthearted laughter, and also manage to work hard. For all of us, international and local, the feeling of helping and sharing together created a rare sense of shared happiness.

"Just a few days after we had arrived, we received word from Fr. Stephan, the local Roman Catholic priest. He invited Father Nithiya to join him in celebrating Mass on Sundays and during various evenings. He explained that he was the sole spiritual caregiver for 50,000 congregants and that his work was becoming overwhelming.

"This was a period when there were critical shortages of active Roman Catholic priests in Hungary and in neighboring nations because many people were using their new freedom to seek answers and quench a deep spiritual thirst.

"Father Nithiya took on double duty, during the day working with the RYS volunteers and, in the evenings, offering Holy Communion to Hungarian congregants.

"A Franciscan and an Indian, Fr. Nithiya found deep inspiration in the lives of two spiritual giants: St. Francis, a Christian, and Mahatma Gandhi, a Hindu. He saw in their lives brilliant examples of what it meant to live for the sake of others. His efforts in Tatabanya, Hungary did not escape the attention of the region's bishop, and he was recognized for his efforts.

"You see, Fr. Nithiya was the right man for the right job at the right time and place, even though we had almost rejected him because he was too old. Not only did he do transformative, important work in Hungary, he went on to serve in India, helping the beautiful young children who were combing through trash for sustenance.

"All that wonderful work for humanity would have been lost if we, or he, had decided he was 'too' something. Please don't decide that about yourself. You may have the unique set of skills that are desperately needed in the right job at the right time.

"It's always difficult to measure the value of service and a specific service project. Sure, if you built part of a clinic, and your departure was followed by hundreds of patients having their medical needs taken care of, that clearly would be a valuable result. Often, however, the results of service projects are not visible or apparent. Service can help heal a heart or grow a relationship where there was none. Service and service projects can help us see life from a new and fuller perspective and lead us toward a lifetime of good action.

"One immeasurable result of service, my friends, is that service makes you happy! The famous Bengali poet, sage, composer, and philosopher, Rabindranath Tagore, insightfully noted this about life and the role of service: 'I slept and dreamt that life was joy. I awoke and saw that life was service. I acted and behold, service was joy.'

"How many of you want to be happy? Yes, I thought so. Everyone. Me too.

"A well-crafted service initiative can provide an environment where volunteers are introduced into an ethos of service. Some discover a deep sense of joy and satisfaction in such an environment and redirect their lives by making service a higher priority. On completing a project, many participants enthusiastically announced that

316

their lives were changed through their experiences. Some moved forward to establish a personal legacy rich in goodwill and humanitarian achievements.

"So, however puny or ineffectual you and your efforts may seem to you, your efforts will count. They will count inside you, giving you joy, and they will count outside of you, helping the community, and maybe having a ripple effect far beyond what you expect.

"Now, how many want to go ahead with your own service project?"

Kyle waved vigorously. Chrissy swallowed and shyly raised her hand. Juan did too. Slowly, one by one, the students sheepishly raised their hands.

"I'm proud of you," said the Grandfather. "An old adage about service is that, in the end, you will receive more—sometimes much more—than you gave. You'll wish you'd done more service by the time you are through. Take heart, my young friends. I know you can do this."

He nodded to Juan, Chrissy, and Kyle, who rose to offer a song to a suddenly calmer and more confident class of young people.

Chapter 24: The Man Who Spoke With His Shovel

"A dream doesn't become reality through magic; it takes sweat, determination, and hard work."

General Colin Powell

"Thank you for last week," Mr. Bennet said to the Grandfather the next time the class met at the elderly gentleman's house. They watched the students settling into their places on the grass. Just as in class, everyone seemed to have selected his or her own little patch to sit on. Students sat in the same place almost every time, and the class observed everyone's claims to various spots. "They do seem a little more open to actually doing projects now."

"They can do one today!" the Grandfather said.

"Words are one thing; deeds are another. There's no better way to teach them than to get them doing!"

"Doing what?" asked Mr. Bennet.

The Grandfather gave him a quick run-down on what he suggested for that afternoon's class.

Mr. Bennet nodded enthusiastically.

"And it's alright with Mrs. Thiset?" he asked.

"She can't wait."

The Grandfather clapped his hands for attention.

"My friends, welcome to all of you. It's always wonderful to see your bright, beautiful, young faces."

The students smiled at the compliment and murmured return ones.

"Did you ever spend a hot summer day digging and digging with a purpose and, in the process, discover how sweaty work can leave you with a feeling of satisfaction and joy? I remember as a young, strong, 15-year-old, as a team of two, we dug two meters deep to unclog a collapsed cesspool on a sweltering, hot day in July. It was hard but honest work, and I was able to earn some needed spending money. Have you ever labored shovel-by-shovel, sweat on your brow, towards a measurable goal? At the end of the day, did your muscles sing out a reminder of the price you were willing to pay to reach your goal? Those feelings were likely accompanied by a quiet sense of accomplishment, as hard work is an important element in molding a successful life. General Colin Powell put it well when he said: 'A dream doesn't become a reality through magic; it takes sweat, determination, and hard work.' We can learn much about ourselves and life when we do not shy away from hard work.

"I appreciate the efforts of men and women who, rain or shine, earn their daily bread through the sweat of their labor. I also have seen and experienced how some people look down on laborers. In reality, manual labor is foundational to every aspect of the lives we enjoy."

The Grandfather picked up a shovel that had been placed near his speaking area.

He raised the shovel and declared, "When held in the right hands, a shovel can speak louder and clearer than the speeches of politicians! This story will explain what such a shovel can say. It is about a man who spoke with his shovel."

"As you know, a group of volunteers from the RYS worked in Das Marinas in the Philippines, building a small bridge. Our team had representatives from 16 nations, but the designated language for communication was English.

"Helping to build the bridge was a young Japanese man whose English was very limited. He was an unassuming young man we called Tak, which was probably short for Takahashi or Takamitsu.

"When we arrived at our worksite, we were welcomed by a series of hot days filled with repetitious labor. We dug soil, put soil in buckets, passed the buckets down a long line of hands, emptied the soil, and repeated the process. For variety, we moved buckets of cement.

"When we had work breaks, they were often filled with lively conversations. Tak's natural shyness and his inability to speak English put a real limit on his verbal interactions. Unfortunately, none of us spoke Japanese, so verbal communication simply was not happening.

"Tak never complained; he kept on schedule; he attended all the programs and team meetings, and remained friendly in his quiet way. It was sad that we could not understand, nor could he express, what was going on inside him.

"Now, when I dig, I do not like to have people dig harder and more effectively than me. I like the feeling of being the best digger, or at least close to the best. I admit it; it's a macho thing. When I was younger, I took some comfort living with the illusion that I was one of the best 'diggers' around.

"Yet quiet, shy Tak—well, he became Demon Tak with a shovel in his hand! Tak would set out digging with an unforgiving intensity, set to the pace of his own unique, internal clock. Some of us foolish challengers went shovel for shovel with him, attempting to take him on.

"'He's just a sprinter,' I thought with a cocky arrogance. I imagined he would fade in a little while, and we big guys would set the tempo for the rest of the morning.

"Tak was not a sprinter. Tak was a high-precision, Japanese machine that functioned on levels we did not know existed. He would start digging in the morning and only stop when we had our official breaks.

"During the breaks, we would hang around in groups and mix with the Filipino engineer students who were also working at the site. Tak did not hang around much or chat. To my vexation, he anxiously finished his snack so that he could get back to work. Tak's inner clock was set; he was the first to head back to work after the breaks, and he maintained that standard. Once the shovel and his hand reunited, they seemed to continue at an unbroken, rapid pace.

"In the first days of our work, we imagined that the heavier food at lunch would metabolically slow him down. No, not Tak. Yet the stress of the humid tropic heat and a partially digested meal served to temper the ambition of Tak's challengers. We restarted work, a little slower and less focused, after lunch. For the work demon, though, lunch simply re-energized him. He continued to move into the afternoon at the same intense pace.

Tak hard at work

"As the workday moved to its close, our muscles no longer responded to our brains, and shovels were transformed into heavyweights. Stirred by a competitive spirit, we managed to drag ourselves on to the merciful end. As we watched Tak finish with a flourish, our only solace was the whimsical hope that Tak would fade tomorrow.

"Day after day, Tak proved our hopes were built on shifting sand. Tak continued to shine. It did not take long for us to recognize that Tak was the bright star of the work galaxy. We initially tried to rationalize why Tak was so much better at this work than all of us, but our incredulity melted and was replaced by growing respect. His quiet ways and his determined example won our admiration.

"This is a lovely thing about healthy competition. You get to see what you and others are made of, and you hopefully succeed in pulling the best out of each other. Without Tak, our standard would have been much lower as a group, and we would have settled for much less from ourselves. We often had to push ourselves beyond our usual limitations because we knew there was one person who was always doing that. It was interesting to see the power one person can exert on a group without saying a word.

"In time, some of us grew to realize why Tak worked so hard. He could not meet us in conversations, and he had difficulty sharing what was inside him, but he could show us he cared by the way he worked. However, what this little story is about is not the great physical work of our teammate Tak; rather, it is about what we all learned from his goodbye.

"For some reason, Tak had to leave our project two days early and return to Japan. We were all gathered in a large room to give Tak a warm send-off. After singing some songs and sharing conversations, we turned to Tak and asked if he would share a few parting words with us. Tak reluctantly walked to the front of the large room, seeming so much more uncomfortable without the shovel in his hand.

"Tak looked around at all our receptive faces. He stood quietly. Something was visibly moving him, something that had been brewing inside. He offered a deep bow of respect and then stood for a long time before breaking his silence. Words started to come out, but they were soon choked off by uncontrollable weeping. Sobbing, tears streaming down the face of this high-precision, Japanese machine, our Demon Tak literally broke down in front of our eyes. It was all too much for him. He hurriedly exited the room to hide his emotions.

"We were amazed at the emotional intensity Tak had shown. If we knew more about the internal nature of Japanese culture, we might have been even more amazed. Japanese men do not show their emotions. Too much emotion is seen as a sign of weakness. Yet, Tak was bursting with emotion. He had so much he was feeling, so much he wanted to say, so much he yearned to express.

After taking a good amount of time, Tak regained the confidence to reappear and give his farewell. Now we saw him as an incredibly special young man whom we were just beginning to understand. He returned to the front of the stage and looked at his friends from all parts of the world. He again broke into uncontrollable sobs. It just was too much; a flood of emotions had burst out, and there was no way to put it back.

"What is happening inside a person is often unfathomable to those around him or her. We realized that this quiet, kind young man was going through experiences that would change his life forever. On the eve of his departure, we got a glimpse of the beauty, strength, and fragility of Tak's soul.

"All that time, the only tool available to him to communicate his sincerity to us was his shovel. Then, as he left, the other tool he had was his tears.

"Without words, we knew for certain how much the project had meant to Tak and how much his heart was in his work of helping the beautiful people of Das Marinas.

"I can say from experience that while digging, all the problems of the world are shrunk to a single objective, i.e., moving that dirt. It is all so refreshingly simple, not complicated like career planning or a highly charged emotional relationship. It's not ethereal like 'Let's make a world of peace'. Digging is a wonderful way to narrow down all our worries and troubles into a simple, singular concern with clearly measurable results. Surely the world needs free thinkers, but what it needs more are free thinkers willing to dig the soil of this earth.

"Are you beautiful young people ready to dig the soil of this earth to help someone else?"

There were slow, solemn nods.

"My friends," he said. "Next door is Mrs. Thiset's garden. The soil needs to be turned over so she can plant her vegetables. Most years, she hires a roto-tilling crew to come do it, but she is an elderly woman on a fixed income, and money is a little tight. What's more, she has been generous with our group, often bringing something wonderful for us to eat made of things from her garden. Are you willing to go next door and dig up some soil for Mrs. Thiset?"

The students looked thunderstruck.

Kyle stood up. "Hand me a shovel!" he intoned.

"Now, there are only a few shovels, so you will have to take turns. I know you are not dressed for a work project, so most of you will only do a shovelful or so. We'll get the garden done, and this will be your first successful service project, at which you turned your own hands to helping someone."

Juan picked up his guitar, for his assignment was to encourage the students with music. The music under Juan's lead picked up its cadence and simulated the hard work of laborers through sound. Repetition and occasional grunts and groans added to the musical backdrop of a song of Juan's own composition about "Working, Working, Working, All the Long Day Long".

Singing along on the easily learned choruses, the students piled into Mrs. Thiset's yard and lined up around her garden. By mutual agreement, the girls started so they could stand along the grassy edges and not wade into the dirt with the delicate fabrics of their shoes and clothing.

They handed the few shovels around, and then the boys got "down and dirty" into the middle of the garden, continuing to work, sing, laugh, and challenge each other as to who could lift the biggest shovel-fulls of dirt.

Soon, the garden was turned over. Mrs. Thiset clasped her hands together in delight.

"Oh, look at all that freshly turned soil! Oh, I'll have a good garden this year! Thank you all! Thank you so much!"

None of the students had complained, and they seemed to be having the time of their lives. The Grandfather and Mr. Bennet were exchanging triumphant glances when Margaret, a very pretty and fashionable girl, cried out.

"I got dirt on my new designer jeans!"

Everyone held their breath in anticipation of the first spirit-puncturing daggers of the complaint.

Then Margaret said, clasping her hands rapturously, "I'm so proud!"

Chapter 25: Wonderful Ones

"Gandhi, you have been working fifteen hours a day for fifty years. Don't you think you should take a vacation?" Gandhi smiled and replied, "I am always on vacation."

Now the students showed more interest and confidence in planning their service projects. Mr. Bennet could trust that they would come to class with well-thought-out reports on how their small groups had fared during the week with ideas, plans, and even the beginnings of implementation.

Juan, Chrissy, and Kyle had decided that their "shovels" were their musical instruments. They were having a hard time deciding where and how to apply music as a service project, though.

Juan decided to drop in on the Grandfather alone after school to ask him his advice. It was relaxing to be alone with the Grandfather one-on-one. Juan explained his dilemma about the service project as he drank tea in the Grandfather's cozy living room.

"For us, making music is so joyful, it's more like fun than hard work."

The Grandfather laughed. "Yet you worked hard to learn how to play so well, and how to read music. As did Chrissy and Kyle, I'm sure."

"That's true," said Juan.

"Physical labor is a great service, but there are other kinds of service too. And service should be joyful. Gandhi considered his work so rewarding, he said he was always on vacation. I'd like to tell you about a young man named Laxmi who was strongly influenced by the words and actions of the great leader Mahatma Gandhi. Laxmi joined our international service project in Italy. Gandhi spoke much about the people labeled 'untouchables' as well as those people and forces who were doing the labeling. Gandhi shared that, 'In battling against untouchability, I have no less ambition than to see a full regeneration of humanity.' Laxmi, our friend who joined us in Italy, was a man who took those words to heart."

Juan was silent. He was pretty sure his father had been on the RYS project in Italy, but he wasn't sure if this was the right time to ask. The Grandfather paused quizzically, though, as if reading his expression, so Juan swallowed and forced out the words.

"Was my father on the project in Rome? I seem to remember him talking about it one time."

"He was there," nodded the Grandfather. "And he was very much part of everything we did there. Our days under the Roman sun were filled with moving bricks and dirt and many other labor-intensive jobs. The worksite welcomed volunteers from Japan, Korea, the USA, Argentina, Venezuela, Korea, India, Ethiopia, South Africa, Italy, Israel, Canada, and the Philippines.

"It was intense. Even though we were young and idealistic, we often carried the weight of our own cultural, racial, and religious prejudices. At times we would get caught, or we would catch ourselves, in our own hypocrisy. The discomfort would push us to look more clearly at ourselves and evaluate what we could do to measure up to our ideals. It was as if we spent the summer cleaning our mirrors, i.e., the mirrors of our souls, as well as doing physical labor.

"Thinking about those volunteers that summer brings certain images to my mind: Daniel, a rabbinical student from Argentina with his good jokes and serious prayers, your father and his guitar, and Laxmi, the social worker from India. Laxmi danced one evening with joyous abandon, carrying an imaginary hand flute in the courtyard of St. Peter's at the Vatican. You see, Laxmi was an enlightened soul, a free man. He was unafraid of so much that most of us fear, especially social pressures.

"Often, Laxmi's efforts to serve drew criticism instead of praise from those he loved the most. Laxmi's heart was most invested in serving the poorest of the poor, those who were classified as the Scheduled Class (the Untouchables). His family belonged to the high Brahmin or priestly class in Hinduism. Brahmins maintain strict purification rites that Laxmi regularly broke while attending to the poor. When visiting his parents, he was required to carry out numerous cleansing rituals before entering his parents' home. They had difficulty understanding why their son was so moved to give up the good things in life for the sake of the poor.

"Although Laxmi loved his parents, he simply loved the essence of goodness in each human soul more. Modeling the change he sought, Laxmi's life provided a visible lesson for those fortunate enough to come into contact with him.

"As unique as his individual qualities were, many other sojourners in our group embodied in their own way those qualities that we wanted to see in society writ large, including your father with his charisma and his ability to charge a whole group with positive energy.

"Our volunteers in Italy shared a special experience with Laxmi while visiting St. Peter's Square on a warm summer evening. This famous site, a symbol of worldwide Christianity, was filled with tourists and pilgrims. Our group's religious diversity—young Sikhs in turbans, Jews wearing yarmulkas, and robed Buddhist monks—attracted the eyes of numerous onlookers.

"Laxmi added to the visual display by joyfully dancing and playing an imaginary flute like the Hindu deity Krishna. We laughed and seemed to catch some of the joyful spirits of Krishna and added our own contributions to this in our own universal celebration of life.

"Laxmi's joy was contagious, as was his zest for life. This is one of the unforgettable images that were planted in our hearts and minds during that summer of service: Laxmi dancing with his invisible flute. This is part of the reason why the surprise of his sudden passing struck us so hard."

"Ohh," said Juan. "I'm sorry."

The Grandfather nodded. "Just two years after we left our work in Italy, many of us were shocked when we heard the bitter news. Our friend Laxmi was dead. We learned that he had contracted a fatal disease while working with the poor in an overcrowded urban area. Working without fear, he visited areas where disease hung close to the hungry child. He saw the needs, not the dangers. What a tragedy it seemed at first that his life was cut short. Yet, on reflection, it would have been sadder if Laxmi did not dare to challenge convention and reach out to serve those in desperate need. His was a life of meaning. It held within its too short years something precious, something that made a difference, something irreplaceable. For that, we were grateful."

"He sounds so good," said Juan.

"There were so many good souls who worked in Italy that summer. Two, a married couple, Henry and Philomena, served as the elders of our worksite and invested their hearts into the people and the work at hand.

Henry had given up his prestigious UN post midway in his career to focus his life work on training 'Untouchable' Christian youth. His efforts to protect the Untouchables included organizing camps and training, writing publications, promoting films, and speaking against the lingering effects of the caste system.

"The Indian government made a great effort to redress the historic mistreatment of the millions of its citizens by creating the Scheduled Class. Those in the Scheduled Class could receive government benefits while others were not able to receive. Yet, Christian Untouchables were not able to receive government benefits because they no longer fit into the Scheduled Class system. While in Italy, Henry brought this issue up to Vatican representatives to solicit their support. He was offering a voice to those who had none.

"I have been blessed to work with many wonderful ones who, to some, seemed ordinary. I have watched them take responsibility to do what others would not or could not do. As a volunteer, Debendra served in the Philippines and returned to his native Nepal with a vision, motivation, and creativity. His work in service and training would be his life-long passion. In Nepal, he began with training designed

337

to help Katmandu's street children repair bicycles. In his life, when he saw a need, he worked to fulfill it. Dr. Marie Renee established an academy and a medical clinic in Haiti based on the needs of native Haitians as well as Haitian immigrant youth living in New York City. Her story is one filled with doing what was not done before and giving all the glory to God.

"Most of these wonderful but ordinary people were moved by their consciences and acted on intuitive inspiration. By doing that, they became leaders. In telling their stories, it is clear to me that good leadership is more than the function of a title or position; good leadership is rooted in a desire to take care of the needs of others so strong, it overrides the body's desire for its own satisfactions and moves us to take action. Actions can speak louder than words, as we see unreliable to those who make empty promises and fail to live up to them.

"Another essential quality of leadership is humility. True humility (not a groveling kind of humility) recognizes our personal value and sees value in others. If you are humble enough to listen, learn, and take risks, you stand a good chance of developing capabilities beyond those of the talented but self-absorbed. Leaders are willing to make

338

sacrifices even when they receive no personal benefit. They maintain a vision, a clear desire, and a willingness to work to bring the results they strive for. Your father was like that," the Grandfather said. "And I see those qualities in you, Juan."

"In me?" Juan was astounded.

"Yes, in you."

The two men, young and old, sipped their tea. Juan was stunned silent. He wanted to deny what the older man had said, query as to whether he really meant it, deflect the largeness of the compliment. Instead, he sat still, trying to absorb it.

Sunset was turning the windows orange with glowing, if fading, light.

"It was coming on to dusk—sunset—when Laxmi danced," the Grandfather mused. "And your father played his beautiful guitar, the notes tempered like the sun's parting rays."

Juan's mind lingered on the image of Laxmi with his invisible flute, dancing like Krishna, a Hindu god. He imagined his father in a Roman square, wielding his guitar.

Then, suddenly, he knew what he was going to do for his service project.

The idea was so overwhelming, his mouth popped open and closed several times as he contemplated it. Would Mr. Bennet allow it? Would Chrissy and Kyle agree? Would he himself—dare?

"Grandfather," he said, grabbing the Grandfather's wrist with a trembling hand. "I think I've got an idea."

"Do tell," urged the Grandfather.

Excitedly, Juan poured out his vision as the Grandfather smiled and smiled, seeming to bask in happiness.

"What do you think?" Juan when he finished triumphantly.

"I think it is brilliant," said the Grandfather. "And a great service."

Juan embraced the old man and then raced out of the house. He almost leaped over the hedge as he was so excited to get—anywhere. Mostly, though, he was excited to get home, gather his thoughts, and call Chrissy and Kyle.

Chapter 26: Aboriginal Angst and Revitalization

"We don't invent our mission; we detect it. It is within us waiting to be realized."

Viktor Frankl

The next time the class met at the Grandfather's, the trio performed at their absolute best. Mr. Bennet had not yet said yes to their project; they were trying to win him over. His expression conveyed nothing.

The rest of the audience certainly appreciated them. The applause was thunderous.

The Grandfather rose to speak.

"Thank you for that spirited performance, Kyle, Chrissy, and Juan. Very beautifully done. You are an inspiration to us. I'm sure you could be an inspiration to many others." He looked at Mr. Bennet and smiled winningly.

"Today, my story is about the original inhabitants of Australia and their relationship to modern Australia.

"Australia today is a nation with an increasingly diverse population: waves of new immigrants, the descendants of colonial settlers, and the indigenous people. This is a land where antiquity and modernity meet—a meeting often more turbulent than tranquil.

"For tens of thousands of years, the Aboriginals of Australia, the continent's original residents, were intricately connected to the rhythms and harmony of nature. They embraced a perception that each person is connected to the earth, the sky, the animals, and even the rocks and rivers. Aboriginal cosmology differs greatly from that of Australia's European settlers.

"A member of the Aboriginal community offered his perspective: 'Our people endeavored to live with the land while they [the settlers] seemed to live off it. We found food where they found none. We were taught to preserve and never to destroy. We had inherited an understanding of life that places each in kinship with all that surrounds us. Our ways were not appreciated nor respected by the early settlers.'

"When European settlers arrived in large numbers in the eighteenth century, they saw themselves as gifting to

Australia great advances in science, commerce, religion, law, transportation, and farming. Yet the Aboriginal people were semi-nomadic, hunter-gatherers; they had not yet

learned how to use metal, nor did they cultivate the land.

"The Europeans had a hunger to own land. They formed the biased conclusion that the Aboriginals lacked the abilities to own and care for the land. Soon, this biased judgment became the basis for laws prohibiting Aboriginal land ownership—laws that continued to be enforced well into the twentieth century.

"The differences between the Aboriginals and the settlers eventually erupted into violence. It was an uneven contest with little doubt about the outcome. In a short span of time, the Aboriginal people fell from the position of noble caretakers to a conquered people.

"Over the years, the spirit of the Aboriginal people suffered from the physical and psychic damage inflicted on them. Generations of Aboriginal children grew up surrounded by a society that alienated them from their cultural roots by forbidding schools to teach the traditional ways or use the native language. Many were forced to live on reservations or in missions. Aboriginals were paid lower wages for their labor, and they were disenfranchised, so the political powers had little concern for their situation. Often, young Aborigines had little to identify with except feelings of alienation and dislocation—which fueled alcoholism within their community.

"Then the 1970s saw a time of great change. Within the Aboriginal community, a new attitude of cultural pride began to blossom with a rediscovery of Aboriginal music and the popularization of Aboriginal art forms. In 1972, voting rights were finally granted to Aboriginals, while public acts of restorative justice increased.

"Then, in April 1975, Australia chose to open its doors to a wave of endangered South Vietnamese immigrants after the Vietnam War. The impact of this generous immigration policy is very visible today, especially in big cities. One out of every four persons living in Australia has come from another country. Australia is transforming into a global nexus point. Increased openness to other cultures has fueled appreciation for Australia's Aboriginal people.

"Michael Jarrett, an Aborigine, spent his youth in the old Australia, and he was also a part of the new Australia. His energetic spirit and creative mind were determined to shape Australia's future constructively for the sake of his children and community.

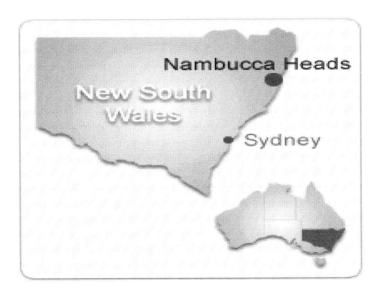

"Each person can achieve greatness. Greatness has more to do with a virtuous character than it has to do with wealth, status, and position. The everyday actions of good people may not make the morning news, but they make a crucial difference in the quality of our lives. People who catch a vision of how things should be and dedicate their hearts, time, and energy toward fulfilling that vision are a powerful force to reckon with. Micklo Jarett, or Michael as we knew him, was such a person.

I met Michael when I traveled to Australia with my colleague, Fazida Razak, to establish RYS in Australia and throughout the South Pacific region. In Sydney, Fazida and I addressed an audience of leaders from a variety of professions gathered by the Universal Peace Federation, our host, and one of our funders.

"We sought to convey how the efforts of RYS worldwide helped inspire personal transformation as well as promote reconciliation and healing. We noted how the RYS model offered experiential insights into substantial ways to meet the challenges of a culture in transition. RYS offered a practical approach to healing historic wounds, such as those inflicted on the Aboriginal communities of Australia.

The audience responded well. Then the spontaneous comments of George Lemon made the deepest impression. Respected for his work in public service and politics, George championed the RYS cause.

"He said, 'As a young man, I decided to take a chance and went to the first RYS project. Those experiences more than a decade ago forever changed my perspective on life. The project made a powerful impact on each participant. We came from 36 nations and a wide range of religious and cultural backgrounds, but we did our best to offer our services to the beautiful people in our community in the Philippines for more than a month.

'I had many concepts about people. Those concepts were challenged when I worked and lived close together with people from every race and religion. The work opened me to a larger understanding of the daily reality that so many people in the world face. I completely changed my attitude. I carried my inspiration into activity and got involved in finding ways to create better relationships between the people of Australia and the Philippines. When more Australians gain this kind of experience, they will be ready to help build a better future for all of us.'

"Immediately following the seminar, two dozen of the conference participants joined a planning meeting organized by Mrs. Aila Willets, a Finnish-born Sydney resident. Like an expectant mother, she made many preparations and hoped to see the inaugural meeting giving birth to an Australian RYS chapter.

"Michael Jarrett was quick to grab hold of the RYS vision; he saw the potential it had for his Aboriginal community of Nambucca Heads. More than a mere dreamer, Michael had a clear sense of what was needed. He

photo courtesy of http://www.rnld.org/

pleaded the case for RYS to launch in his community. Those present, sensing the urgency of his commitment,

agreed. RYS would begin in Nambucca Heads, and Michael would be the program's first Australian project director.

"Not yet 40 years old, Michael was full of energy and hope. He was the proud father of six children and a faithful husband and friend to his wonderful wife. Michael owned a clunker of a car, and he possessed little. Yet Michael loved his community and was proud of its strengths while being aware of its weaknesses.

"Nambucca Heads residents were nearly all Aboriginal, and they struggled with many of the challenges facing other similar communities. The painful impact of high underemployment and alcoholism was visible. Vulnerable teenagers, susceptible to destructive behavior patterns, short on self-esteem, struggled to find something to be proud of. For many, it was an environment where it was easy to lose motivation and difficult to envision a future.

"Michael's hope was to provide a positive alternative for those at risk. This was not an easy task. A wounded community is not easily moved. Despite the difficulties, Michael's belief in the power of community was rooted in the ways practiced by his forebears.

"He set out to create a haven for the Nambucca Heads community to meet. He saw the haven as a place where the elders could pass on traditional games and stories, while the young could build friendships and share in enriching and fun activities. The haven would be a place where each person could find moments of inner peace and pride in the community.

"The first major step in Michael's plan was to bring a group of volunteers from other communities, even from other countries, to the area. The volunteers would then paint murals over the graffiti that covered the local bus stop and clear off and equip an area for a children's playground. As a father of six children, Michael knew that the area needed to be fun for children.

"Michael was hopeful that, by introducing bright, young volunteers, the community could gain fresh perspectives on the possibilities for positive change as well as experience a renewed sense of cultural pride.

"In the intense heat of the Australian summer, the service teams worked on clearing the land and creating the beginnings of a community park. A covered, open-air building that served as a bus stop was carefully painted. Together, the teams created the designs and painted several beautiful, cross-cultural murals.

"Community members lost their shyness as the work progressed. Several local youths came to the worksite each day to help. The project became a growing attraction for curious young children. Of course, this drew numerous mothers to the worksite. Elders would also come to offer encouragement and advice. The Elders, who cherished many stories in their hearts, found this a wonderful time to indulge in nostalgia and share. The newcomers found themselves treated to insightful and often colorful narratives. We were all starting to really enjoy each other's company.

"Michael recognized the growing level of trust as a significant achievement. After the successful conclusion of the first project, he invited RYS back for a follow-up. By the time, the third Nambucca Heads project occurred, Michael's reputation was spreading to neighboring communities and beyond. He was awarded nationwide recognition by a major Aboriginal organization. Michael also received an appointment to become an Ambassador for Peace, an honor he took much pride in. Yet Michael maintained the same great sincerity of heart as he continued to drive his old car from destination to destination in his unremitting efforts to promote the community-based projects. Michael personally raised over $4,000 for the third RYS project.

Michael's wife and older children greatly supported his efforts, generously volunteering their time. Through their actions, the Jarrett family provided a rallying point for the community, and they helped to stimulate others' contributions to the public good.

"On the morning of the opening day of the third project, participants anxiously awaited the delivery of materials. A large truck pulled into the area, and the volunteers and community members quickly sprang into action to unload it. There is a strength, an undeniable power that arises when a community works for a singular purpose.

"Our mutual respect grew when the curious volunteers queried members of the community about their culture and history. A mother showed us how to make music using the leaves of a local tree. Some of the men shared insights on survival skills that were a vital part of growing up in a traditional Aboriginal community.

"The learning process went in both directions. Asian and American participants were showered with questions about their lifestyles and interests. A Korean volunteer-created unity by pointing out that many of their shared musical interests transcended national and cultural borders.

"As the week in Nambucca Heads neared its close, community members wanted us to share a fun and memorable goodbye. They organized an evening cultural program. Cultural programs are often one of the best parts of RYS because they provide participants and community members a time to share their hearts and talents. As an act of love, a great deal of effort was invested in preparing songs, dances, skits, and other homegrown entertainment.

"That night, we were treated to traditional Aboriginal music, Korean songs, some skits, and several emotional testimonies. While many of the local folks expressed tearful gratitude to RYS, RYS participants, in their turn, shared how the people of Nambucca Heads had shown them the true meaning of community.

"At one point, the local Catholic priest, Father Tony, grabbed his guitar and serenaded the audience with some folksy songs that got the group going. The next day, he confessed to Fazida that the cultural night was the first celebration he had ever been to in Nambucca Heads, where there was no drinking or fighting and where everyone had a great time. It was a milestone for the community.

"A few of the volunteers returned a year later to visit. Some were afraid that they would find the murals damaged by graffiti and the haven and gazebo in disuse and disrepair. Yet, as our van turned and we reached the bus stop, the untouched murals radiated a feeling of a warm welcome. The haven was clean and was being used well.

"In a private conversation, a couple of teenagers shared:

'We still like to drink, but we don't drink in the haven. The community worked hard to create this special space. It is like a sacred area . . . The murals are more than paintings, for they represent our shared friendship.'

"Michael Jarrett, one man, driven by love for his people, ennobled and engaged others in a vision they made their own. The results he brought were not based on his economic status, education, or well-connected friends. It was the wonderful power of one committed individual."

Chapter 27: The Politics of a Mother's Heart—Mama Betty Style

"A mother holds her child's hand for just a short time, but holds their hearts forever."

Krystal Nahdee

Kyle, Chrissy, and Juan launched into their performance. This gathering had a distinctive flavor because of the music offered by several special guests. Juan knew that the Grandfather was going to be sharing about Africa, and he remembered that his father had once been friends with some men in an African band. He had asked them to help set the tone for the upcoming talk.

Some of the guest musicians brought African instruments, string, wind, and percussion. Kyle, Chrissy, and Kyle enjoyed finding spots to blend into the less familiar sounds, using their creativity and musical craft. They had once presented their version of African music to the group; this was so much better.

Mr. Bennet had not given permission for the trio to do their proposed project yet. Juan was always performing for Mr. Bennet, trying to win his approval. This time, though, Juan forgot that worry. He loved music; he loved "jamming" with musicians with other styles; Chrissy and Kyle were in festive spirits, and the music was taking off. He lost himself in it, sharing joyfully in the mysterious oneness that sometimes comes up between fine performers and their audiences. Many of those sitting on the grass were interacting with the music, joining in on repetitive verses, making dancing gestures with their arms, or clapping along in rhythm. Like a growing chorus in anticipation of a great event, the feelings and sound grew. It all ended in a

satisfying crescendo, and then everyone burst into applause.

Smiling and clapping, the Grandfather assumed his place on the grassy prominence and expressed his appreciation to the musicians for evoking the beauty of Africa. Then he launched into his story.

"I paused on a hill one morning," the Grandfather began, "and I gazed at a horizon of green rolling hills and long stretches of fertile fields. The timeless beauty, enhanced by the sounds of nature's ever-active song, was a comfort to my spirit. Just a year earlier in Uganda's Lira District, the secure blanket of the morning's calm would have been ripped apart by the peppering of gunfire.

"For ages, Lira was a serene land where peace was the norm, but political upheaval had fomented waves of violence and unrest. This day, the fresh and clear air, blue sky, and open vistas offered a perfect setting to reflect on how the recent transformation to tranquility had come about.

"Often, at critical times, special people rise to help shape events. The efforts of these individuals, even just their timely presence, can provide a calming impact and shed light on possible alternatives to conflict. When I recall the peaceful transition that occurred in Lira, it is Mama Betty Okwea's image that comes to my mind. Minister Okwea—or Mama Betty, as we affectionately called her—embodied a heart and character that could placate the angry, stimulate the listless, and offer hope to the hopeless. Mama Betty's leadership was shaped by her deep love for the people and her endless willingness to serve her war-torn nation.

"

"Flag of Uganda" by Tobias

"Uganda is a land blessed with many natural and human resources. Located near the center of Africa, it borders no ocean. In a way, her geography helped spare her from the harshest aspects of slavery so prevalent along the coastal regions of Africa. The world's largest river, the Nile, finds its origin in this region; its source, Lake Victoria, covers a large part of Uganda's southeast border. The nation spans lush tropical forests, temperate mountain regions, and semiarid plateaus filled with cattle, herders, and the occasional poacher. It is the home of some of the most beautiful sights in the world.

"The capital city of Kampala, with well over a million residents, was built on the wooded 'Hills of the Impala.' The city's elevation spares it from the harsh heat that often bakes cities close to the equator.

"In 1962, British colonial rule ended, followed by a time of promise and hope.

Yet many of the dreams of the newly independent nation swiftly turned into nightmares. A series of despotic rulers left as their legacies war, violence, and misrule. President Milton Obute was one of the world's worst violators of human rights. His harsh rule was ended by a coup. Unfortunately, the new leader, Idi Amin, imposed his own brutal sovereignty for eight years. Under Amin, more than 300,000 citizens were summarily executed, and Uganda's large and successful East Indian population was pushed into exodus. The ethnic Indians, Ugandan citizens, had been a critical cornerstone of the nation's economy, and they also provided fine examples of family cooperation. With their departure, a precious vital force disappeared.

"Coat of arms of the Republic of Uganda" by Sodacan

"During these two decades of turbulent misrule, the good people of Uganda shed many tears. Fortunately, the 1990s marked a period of transformation and greater stability as a former rebel leader, Yoweri Museveni, became the nation's president. Museveni helped rein in much of the violence. In spite of some conflict with ethnic rivals in neighboring Rwanda and Congo, Museveni's rule was a period of relative domestic calm and economic development.

"Yet, another killer began to take away the nation's young and promising. The AIDS virus struck across tribal lines, and fighting its spread required cooperation between civil society, the government, and all tribal groups. Fortunately, Ugandans rose to the challenge, with religious leaders, health workers, educators, and non-government organizations all working cooperatively.

"The Ugandan people had strong religious sensitivities; there was an almost universal acknowledgement of a transcendent God. While 85% of the population followed Christianity, a substantial Muslim minority often lived and worked side by side. Hindus and Sikhs among the returning East Indians, and the Bahai religion, which chose Uganda as one of its worldwide centers, added to the mix. Some traditional African forms of worship linger also. The nation's strong spiritual foundation, highlighted by its respect for religion, has afforded its people remarkable resilience.

"The RYS and the International Relief Friendship Foundation (IRFF) were invited to take part in a variety of service projects spanning several years. Some of those efforts involved repairing schools, while others were aimed at improving local medical facilities and substantially enhancing local agricultural techniques.

"When I first arrived in Uganda in 1999, I discovered vibrancy and freshly distilled optimism. The fear that had gripped the nation for two decades, oppressing many aspects of daily life, had largely dissipated. A nationwide restructuring and decentralization of authority had served to empower local communities, restoring a sense of hope and promise. Many citizens were feeling that their voices were being heard and that they, once again, had the power to shape their destinies.

"The resurgence of greater political freedom was accompanied by a revitalization of the economy and a renewed sense of national pride. Substantial efforts were being made to heal and repair past damage.

"When we first arrived in the Lira district, we RYS volunteers noticed military trucks patrolling the roads. Possibly to calm our nerves, we were told that the military presence was more a precaution than a necessity. Even more noticeable, though, were the Lira District school children in their bright, neat uniforms, making their way to school in the mornings. Laughter and conversation could be heard as they walked, often in small groups, down paved and unpaved roads. The sounds of lively school children in the mornings were a clear sign that daily life was settling back into a more natural and carefree routine.

"With normalcy reasserting itself, preserving the peace was a foremost concern of those living in the district. It is during such times that good leadership is critically needed. The Lira region was served well by a special leader—Mama Betty Okwea.

"Mama Betty stood almost six feet tall, and her big-boned frame was assuredly helpful for carrying the extra love she held in her heart. Mrs. Betty Okwea was the Minister to the Vice President of Uganda, and she was a true people's politician. Though often carried out quietly behind the scenes, her efforts were part of the reason people in the district were turning their backs on violence. She was working hard to help the community regain a positive vision for the future. It was also through her strong encouragement that our group chose to work in Lira.

"Minister Okwea understood human nature. She realized that each person needs to be listened to and that all of us have a yearning for recognition. A leader's indifference may generate resentment and frustration in the governed. It is the frustrated people—those who see no hope in the future, those who hear the daily cries of hungry children—who become most liable to lash out.

"The frustrated anger of men in a house is often unleashed on those close to them, their vulnerable family members. Also, Minister Betty understood that frustrated people are much more prone to take up arms against their government than those who feel respected.

"The minister approached people with a natural concern that enabled each to feel that he or she was important. All the people were, indeed, important to Mama Betty. She paid attention to each person's needs, bestowing respect upon each. Her style was to comfort rather than confront.

"To meet the needs of her often-demanding constituents, Minister Okwea had to model patience and a down-to-earth humility. Yet, this quality of humility went far beyond passive acceptance. When the situation required it, she would act forthrightly, taking the dynamic initiative to serve the people's needs.

"Mama loved traveling through the various districts in Uganda, but her home base in the Lira District was where she was most free. I was fortunate to join her in traveling with a small group that included Uganda's two national ministers for youth. They were a young man and a young woman who represented Uganda's youth in the nation's parliament. In my eyes, this was an exciting advance in governing because it gave young people a clear voice in the debates and decisions of the country.

"Our small team moved from village to village, meeting groups of people—a youth meeting at one stop, a gathering at a mosque at another. Visits to schools and clinics were also part of Mama Betty's busy daily schedule.

"Within a day of traveling and meeting people with Minister Okwea, I began developing a deep appreciation of her work with constituents. Meeting and greeting are a normal part of the lives of elected officials, but Minister Okwea showed us the hard work and care that is involved in doing this service well. Mama Betty listened to people's stories and heard their requests, promising to address critical issues. I was amazed at her patience as she listened to the many requests and complaints.

"My reaction was vastly different than Mama's. I wondered, almost out loud, 'What do these people expect from her? Does the minister look like a magical parent or Santa Claus? Why are they asking for so many things that they could take responsibility for themselves?'

It seemed to me that whole communities were awaiting a magic wand to transform their lives. I have come across this attitude in other parts of the world, too, so perhaps it is universal. But I wondered as we drove the dusty roads if the people would ever realize the power that lay within their own grasp. I wondered if they would ever understand that they had the ability to make much more of a difference in their own lives than the government ever could.

"When we arrived at the next community—one somewhat poorer than the previous ones—we were guided to the local mosque. The light blue sky was painted with clusters of white clouds as we met outside a simple mosque. A group of men approached Minister Betty as if pleading a case in front of a judge. They complained about various things, but the highlight of the grievances was that the new, modern mosque had been left three-quarters finished. The foreign donors from a Gulf country were no longer sending money to the community.

"Those gathered were vocal and upset, demanding that the Uganda government finish the job of building the mosque. I saw Mama nod and listen even as I grew more and more aggravated. I felt like shouting at the people, 'If this is your mosque, then work together and finish it on your own! Stop complaining! Take responsibility! Why should the government do what you can do yourselves?'

"I held things inside until after the meeting adjourned and the men had made their way back down the dirt road toward the village. I did tell Mama what I felt, and she nodded at me with the patient nod I had seen her give to complaining villagers. I was being given a dose of Mama's medicine.

"Then she said, 'I have to listen to these people because no one else does. They may be trying to get something from us that we cannot give, but at least they know we came and showed an interest in them. This is what most people need. They need to know someone is listening to them, that someone cares. Even though they really don't expect you to solve their problems, they appreciate anything you can do to help.

"Mama Betty looked drained from all the travel and meetings, but she continued. 'I often feel like a mother with many children. As a mother, I realize that the food in the pantry is not enough to fully satisfy the children, so I simply must do my best. I listen to their dreams, encourage them by saying that things will get better, and I do whatever little I can.' She suddenly smiled with her whole face and laughed out loud. 'Fortunately, we Ugandans are a hopeful people!'

"Hearing this important government minister share her heart of concern was a lesson for me. It is a lesson that should not be lost among our own political leaders. Seeing Mama Betty in action, it was clear that she was a much bigger person than I was. Part of her special legacy is that she has helped me and others grow in our hearts to become bigger and better people with her simple wisdom that people need to be listened to, to be heard, and to know that someone cares. That may be the greatest service."

Chapter 28: A Royal Example

"Eternal gratitude towards the past.
Unlimited service in the present
Unbounded responsibility for the future."
Huston Smith

It had happened. Mr. Bennet had given the musical trio permission to do their service project. They were starting it this very morning.

A short student named Nathan came along with them to the subway station. He had been at loose ends, unable to fit into a group, so they had added him to theirs as the video recorder.

They were nervous but excited. They decided to let Chrissy do the introductions.

"Like Mama Betty," Kyle said. "They'll trust their hearts more to a woman."

There were many people crowded on the subway. It was 8:00 a.m., and many people were on their way to work. Most looked tired and gloomy. Some were tooling around on their cell phones; others stared straight ahead unseeingly so as not to attract or give unwanted attention.

"Good morning!" said Chrissy loudly. She smiled, and several people stared at her. Some looked annoyed, some obviously were thinking she was crazy, and yet others looked admiring. "We're from the high school, and as our service project to the community, we've going to serenade you! I know a lot of you are already listening to things on your phones, but if you give us an ear, we're hoping it will brighten up your day. There's nothing like live music, after all."

She fell back into line between Juan and Kyle, who began singing and playing "The Rainbow Connection." Some people laughed in recognition, murmuring about Kermit the Frog. Others turned away with surly, scared, or sullen looks on their faces.

The trio gave it their all. To their delight, some people began to sing along, which they encouraged with smiles and nods. For a moment, Juan thought the subway car was actually rocking in rhythm as most of the people ultimately joined in, especially on the choruses, and smiles broke out all along the rows of seated people.

"Thank you so much!" called out Juan when the song was over. "It was our pleasure to share music with you, and we hope everyone has a wonderful day today."

They got off at the stop in front of their high school, resisting the impulse to burst into laughter or sounds of joy.

Nathan said, "Wait till Mr. Bennet sees this video! Practically everyone on the subway went from a frown to a smile."

At the Grandfather's that afternoon, the trio asked everyone to watch their video on YouTube. Cries of delight arose from the students as they watched the public's reaction to the subway minstrels. Mr. Bennet seemed pleased, and when Juan held his cell phone in front of the Grandfather for him to watch, the elderly gentleman crowed with delight and applauded.

Then he rose to tell his story.

"Maybe there is no better service than to bring smiles to the faces of those who were not happy before you came along. Each of us has the power to do that. I cannot over-emphasize how powerful the example of one person is. As it happens, the person in today's story was a recognized leader, so his actions resonated a great deal, but if anyone doubts that Chrissy, Kyle, and Juan were leaders this morning, I disagree!

"Today's story will take us thousands of miles away, to the beautiful beaches of the island of Tonga, where we will hear about an exceptional leader. First, let me share with you words to reflect on by my former advisor, Dr. Huston Smith. He calls on us to embody:

"Eternal gratitude towards the past.
Unlimited service in the present
Unbounded responsibility for the future."

"The Kingdom of Tonga, once known as the Friendly Islands, contains 176 lush tropical islands that cross the international dateline. The culturally rich Polynesian kingdom was never colonized by Europeans, but they welcomed Christianity. Today 98% of its citizens belong to a church. In the capital city, Tongatapu, an

expression of that faith can be observed each Sunday morning as groups of white-clad ladies stroll, almost parade-like, down the street to attend church.

"Tongans love to sing, and coming together provides a good reason for the song. A person at a gathering will feel moved by the spirit and pick a song to sing; often, it is a religious song. Those gathered may be from different villages and churches but, when they sing together, it is as if they were raised on the same songbook. Their voices naturally fill the air with beautiful, layered harmony.

"Dancing, or Mafana, as it is known in the islands, may follow the singing because it also is a rich aspect of the Tongan culture. To many, Mafana is an expression of pure spiritual exhilaration and has a sacred element to it. The values and traditions of the islands are enriched by song and dance and provide a continuity linking the past to the present.

"In contrast to those in the glamour industry who consider thin to be vogue, the life-loving Tongans have their own standard of beauty. Tongans can be huge, really round. Being a big papa and especially a big mama is an honor, a thing to strive for. When girls reach their middle-teens, they are often encouraged to put on extra weight. Adding weight is like adding some extra beauty.

"The Kingdom of Tonga is governed by a long succession of hereditary rulers. The king and members of the royal family are regarded with respect and near-veneration. They carry with their titles important responsibilities in guiding and governing the country. The example royalty provides of great importance to the nation.

"When royalty behaves with petty self-interest, it can bring disorder. Yet, when they behave in the interests of the people, blessings flow. From my perspective, true royalty is more than a circumstance of birth. It must be coupled with a nobility of character.

"I met and shared with several prominent Tongan Ambassadors for Peace at international conferences. In informal conversations, these leaders enjoyed promoting the unique qualities of Tonga and its people but, when the talks became serious, they would inevitably move to an issue that weighed heavily on them: the values confusion that young people were experiencing in the islands.

"The Tongan elders shared their apprehension that the traditional values of the islands, richly influenced by Christianity, were being challenged by secular, materialistic, and hedonistic influences. They saw the onslaught of outside media as an invading force with the power to move young people in a dangerous direction. Anxious about the future, they sincerely asked for help in protecting the youth and the culture that they loved.

"Moved by this honest appeal, we formulated a plan that garnered support from RYS, the Tongan Family Federation and local Ambassadors for Peace. While researching how to implement an effective program in Tonga, we discovered that the island's churches focused almost exclusively on their own congregations. Any plan we made would need to pull people from the various churches together for the purpose of tackling a mutually agreed-on objective.

"We recruited Mr. Paul Savor, an Australian educator who worked throughout the South Pacific on character-building programs for young adults. Together, we created an interactive program aimed at appealing to a diverse audience. The ecumenical, multi-generational, two-day program offered character education training together with a service project. We also provided time for community members to brainstorm, discuss, and come to a consensus on ways to improve their community. A good amount of time was set aside for singing!

"Paul and I arrived by plane in Tonga and met with the local organizing team. We were happy to be in such a beautiful environment, but we began to grasp the sense of isolation that could be felt living so far from any large landmass. Young people in Tonga were very aware of the larger world, and many suffered from a feeling of being confined. Surprisingly, the island could appear in the minds of its citizens to be a prison, not a paradise. We needed to help the residents rediscover the potential that existed on the islands.

"The Tonga RYS program attracted 60 representatives of social and civic organizations, churches, and various schools. Within the limited time we had together, it was important that we work meaningfully together on a fixable problem. To do this, we had to solicit each person's ideas, form a consensus on which problem to tackle, make a step-by-step plan, and then work cooperatively to accomplish the task in the given time frame.

"The problem of litter on the beaches was an obvious choice. Many of the white sand beaches of the main island were strewn with ugly plastic bottles and various forms of litter. When a beach has a litter on it, it becomes easy for others to add their litter. In time, litter becomes the norm, an accepted fact of life. Cleaning a beach is a good service, but if that work stimulates a change in attitudes towards littering, it makes a more lasting impact.

"We were hoping to create a new attitude and stimulate creative approaches to caring for the environment. Perhaps in the future, one of the volunteers would investigate creating a biodegradable container made from local palm or banana leaves. Such a product could save money, help the environment, and end the overuse of plastic. Progress towards solving this and other problems can be realized when a community works together.

"Early in the morning, before we began our cleanup, we gathered and had an educational session on environmental issues. We took time to solicit feedback about which beaches we would target and how best to keep those areas clean after the cleanup. Before the tropical sunburned too bright, we closed our meeting and began moving to the beaches. Traveling by foot, car, and a pickup truck, with gloves and garbage bags in hand, we headed for the white sand.

"When Lord Baron Vaea, the special advisor to the king, heard of our plans, he loaned us his pickup truck to help collect and move the piles of garbage. The baron, a member of the royal family, was an Ambassador for Peace, a man of heart and character. His support reflected the appreciation he felt for the volunteers and their efforts.

"In ancient China, the emperor would make an annual trip to the countryside during spring planting time. On a piece of farmland, he would take a hoe and make a few cuts in the soil. This was a ritual act done to symbolize solidarity between the emperor and the millions of farmers in his kingdom.

"On the morning of our project, the Lord Baron Vaea came to the beach with the truck and a national TV crew. Our dear baron did more than symbolically pick up a can or two. This huge man bent down and worked as hard as the young volunteers, picking up bag after bag of garbage.

"As a group, we started our physical work with a fresh, bright spirit. We felt invincible; we were new-age warriors and the enemy to be conquered was the garbage. Yet, in time, the heat of the morning increased with the direction of the sun. We were beginning to ache, and our spirits started to gradually sag as we pushed ourselves on.

Then, like a rallying cry from a sergeant in the army, a young lady shouted, 'Shame on us! How can we slow down? Look at how hard Baron Vaea is working!'

"On hearing the admonition, we all started to refocus our efforts. We began singing more and encourage each other. As the day progressed, our bags piled high in the pickup truck. We now could clearly see what this beach area was meant to look like.

"We learn best when we have a good example. Every nation needs good models of leadership if they are to rise above mediocrity. True leaders are those that recognize problems and work on solutions. A true leader will serve, train, motivate and educate others on how to solve problems. Creatively preparing a new generation for leadership allows our society to show gratitude to the past, serve the present, and take responsibility for the future.

"The baron loved the natural beauty of the island, and he wanted the upcoming generation to be able to share his sensitivity and concern. He realized that having a group of people clean up the beach would not prevent it from becoming littered again. What was needed was education, and that education had to begin with an example.

"The best anti-littering education statement in the kingdom was the example of this huge, elder, honored member of the royal family. Those who saw him in person or watched him on national television—sweating, bending, and picking up the litter left by thoughtless acts of disregard—were deeply moved. We were sure all would think twice before littering again.

"My friends," concluded the Grandfather. "You may not be a member of a royal family. Yet each of you can serve as a leader by setting a good example. Just as Chrissy, Kyle, and Juan experienced this morning, people will follow the lead of a person who puts himself or herself out there to benefit others. In fact, the world is waiting for just such people."

Chapter 29: Melinda's Heart

"Love always requires courage and involves risk."

M. Scott Peck

Chrissy and Juan arrived at the Grandfather's a few minutes before everyone else. It was to be their last formal meeting with him before the service projects would take up the full class time. Juan and Chrissy felt a little sad.

"Oh, Juan!" said the Grandfather cheerily. "I've something to show you."

Juan looked at the photograph the Grandfather held. It was his father; young, slender, with lots of hair. Juan's heart thumped in recognition. His father's head was thrown back, and his mouth was open in song as he strummed his guitar. His eyes were closed as if he were in rapture at the music.

"That was in Rome," said the Grandfather gently. "And look at this. One of the neighbors snapped this while you were performing here."

The Grandfather showed him another photo. Juan's eyes widened. It was him, in the exact same posture as his father: slender, with lots of hair, his head thrown back and his mouth open, singing and strumming. The resemblance was so total, Juan felt chills go up and down his spine.

"You see," said the Grandfather, "his legacy lives on."

Juan couldn't help it; emotions coursed through him in a wave so powerful, it had to burst the confines of his body. He wept, trying to choke back the sobs, but the Grandfather patted him on the back, encouraging him to "Let it out." Chrissy tactfully left them alone together, murmuring something about work in the kitchen.

When the flood was over—half of it was taking place on the Grandfather's shoulder—Juan wiped his eyes and struggled to gain control of his voice.

"You've done so much for me," he choked. "Thank you."

"Ah, Juan. You've no idea what you and your fellow students have done for me. Time and seasons pass— including the seasons of youth, maturity, and age—yet things of true and lasting value continue to find expression. When you and your friends first began to visit, the ache deep in my heart turned to joy as I found people with whom to share the stories I treasure, to whom I could bequeath the inheritance of service. These stories are my legacy, and the students are my heirs. It is a relief to me to know this heritage will not go to waste, just as I am sure it is a relief to your father to see you blossoming in service to others through your music."

An unfathomable smile graced the Grandfather's face as he closed his eyes, seeming to quietly thank the source of love, God.

He continued, "Someday, you too will pass on stories and a tradition of service to your own children and grandchildren. It is the hope of the elder for the younger borne out of love. You helped me fulfill that hope."

Chrissy was standing quietly in the doorway.

"Grandfather?" she asked. "May I meet with you after you share your story?"

The elder responded with a cheerful, "It will be my pleasure. May I know our topic of discussion?"

Chrissy ducked her head as if she realized she was a visible display of her feelings and quickly responded.

"I received two letters yesterday saying that my applications to two colleges of my choice were accepted. One acceptance came from a well-known engineering school, with a generous financial aid package and a partial scholarship. Initially, I felt a big ego boost, but now I am coming down to earth and thinking about the difficult decisions I need to make. Do I really want to study engineering? How does going to this school fit in with my future goals and plans?"

"Who was the other acceptance letter from?" the Grandfather asked, echoing Juan's thought.

"It was from a small, not-so-famous college that couldn't offer as much financial aid, but that has a really good work-study program to work things out. It's a music college. I would like to talk with you, Grandfather, even before discussing it with my parents or my counselor. Thank you in advance for making the time for me." She gave the elder a warm smile and then moved off to help those who were setting up on the tables.

After a sweet musical number performed by Chrissy, Juan, and Kyle, the Grandfather assumed his speaking place on the lawn.

"Dear friends, my heart honors the people and the times of service in the Philippines. It is there that my companions and I rediscovered our purpose in life. We learned how, at times, a good heart could be more valuable than all the heads in the world and how we each have a role to play in adding grace and dignity to life.

"Through our efforts to serve, we came to discover a deep joy and the fullness of life. We become, in a sense, the hands, the voice, the expression of God's love.

"The early morning heat, so common in the poor Philippine community of Das Marinas, served as a realistic reminder of the past five weeks of sweaty labor that our international team of volunteers had undertaken. Looking at the colorful, freshly painted International Bridge of Love, I was proud. Thoughts of our everyday challenges were fresh, and the sight of the bridge brought vivid reminders of how hard we had worked as individuals and as a community: the mixing and moving of tons of cement, the constant landscaping, assisting the young Philippine engineers, and all our shared efforts. The concrete structure of our little bridge served as a measure of the progress we had made through our labor.

"In my mind's eye, though, I thought a more subtle and profound measure of progress was in our sense of community. We arrived in Das Marinas as strangers. For many, it was the first time traveling to a new country; for some, it was the first extended stay away from home and family. From morning through night, our group lived, slept, worked, and ate together. Strangers were transformed into friends, and friends became as close as family members.

"Despite our many external differences, we maintained a mutual respect for one another's spiritual values. Coming from so many different countries and backgrounds stimulated us to invest consciously in building personal relationships. Somehow, we gained a sense that our community was like a global family. This feeling was facilitated by our sharing a noble vision, and maintaining that vision helped us commit to a lifestyle that was true to all of our highest values.

"The Filipinos were all very warm and friendly. Within a short period of time, we were adopted as members of the Das Marinas community.

"As I've mentioned, on our final day in Das Marinas, the governor, the bishop, and a local imam joined the community in a ribbon-cutting ceremony to officially open the bridge. That was exciting. Yet, despite the excitement, a cloud of melancholy hung over some of us as we began to grasp the reality of our approaching departure from this community we had grown to love.

"Melinda was having an especially difficult day. A bright, slender college graduate from Iowa, Melinda knew well the ways and lifestyle of middle America. For this all-

Figure 2: Melinda and Sonia

American girl on her first international experience, arriving at Das Marinas provided her with unexpected, face-to-face challenges. She was able to adjust creatively to turn those challenges into a life-enriching experience. For example, while Melinda was a member of the bucket brigade — a long line of volunteers that passed dirt and cement across a sloping terrain during the building of the bridge — she saw other opportunities to express her heart of care and concern more fully.

"Melinda soon realized that her joy was multiplied when she spontaneously shared with the people of the community. During her busy days, Melinda managed to find time for conversations with mothers in front of their homes or to initiate an exchange of ideas with a Philippine college student or visit and present some special offering for the children at the local primary school.

"Through her interactions in the community, Melinda learned about the issues and challenges that confronted local families. She was surprised to discover that many of the female engineering students who worked with us would soon graduate and leave their homes for jobs as maids in Hong Kong or in a wealthy Gulf nation. The weight of debt and the lack of good local employment opportunities created a situation where they would postpone dreams of a career or family for the lonely job of a domestic servant in a foreign county. Melinda was deeply moved.

"Her friendly smile and palpable concern opened doors in the community. She received invitations from radio stations. Some of us could slip away from the worksite during breaks and share a snack with local families because she had been there first. During her visits to the local schools, the children's faces often filled with smiles, and the classrooms reverberated with laughter.

"Melinda could not bear the thought that too soon these smiling, bright children would be pushed out of school into some numbing form of low-paying, menial work. Melinda began to dream of better things for these girls.

"Melinda established one incredibly special relationship. Each day, Sonia, an undersized, undernourished three-year-old girl, could be seen clinging to Melinda. These two grew closer and closer with each passing day. Often, we would see them together, sometimes sharing food or a tired Sonia being carried in Melinda's arms.

"Melinda's time in Das Marinas was nearly over. Iowa, with her wide-open fields deep in the heartland of America, would soon be welcoming her back. A sense of disconnect arose in Melinda during those final hours in her new community. These two worlds existed almost a lifetime away from each other. It was not clear in her thinking how she was going to connect those worlds, but she knew she had to.

"On our final day in the community, Melinda held Sonia, the little girl with big eyes and a dirty face. Melinda's hands and body offered physical comfort and shelter—an expression of the maternal heart that each child has a right to experience. Evident on Melinda's face was the realization that soon she would be leaving this vulnerable child. It was as if, with each step, she was pouring her love into the child's invisible storage tank. Her steps bore a hope that the little one would draw from this tank in the days and months ahead. This was her last chance to see and hug little Sonia, and she had no way of explaining her upcoming departure. Sonia, who had been lifted by Melinda's love, would soon be dropped. Leaving such a vacuum in the child's life was almost too much for Melinda to bear.

"At one point during our closing afternoon, while hundreds of community members and volunteers mixed in noisy celebration of the bridge's opening, Melinda and I walked toward a van that was parked on the side of the road. We had memories of crowding into this van, filling it with the sounds of conversations, song, and laughter, but this was not the time for that. The dam of emotions seemed about to burst. This was to be the quiet sanctuary where we would let the waters flow.

"Away from the crowds, the chaotic sounds, and the children's animated faces, we found our chance. We had a sense this was going to happen, but we could never have anticipated its intensity. The silent van opened the floodgates for us.

"We wept unrestrainedly, an unfamiliar force of emotion shaking our bodies. Varied levels of pained sounds forced their way out of our throats. A moment of silence was followed by quiet sobs and then thunderous sobs of torrential force. The cycle of sounds continued — silence, sobs, and then the torrents — on and on till the water and emotions were all drained out of us.

"We were weeping for all the sorrow of Das Marinas, the dim futures of the children, the challenges of poverty and broken families that weighed heavily on children like Sonia. We were weeping for the doors that education opened that would prematurely slam shut because of Sonia's lack of what was mere pocket money in the United States. Sonia's presence served as an emotional catalyst opening us to the bitter realization that children in thousands of other communities needed love, care, and attention.

Some of the tears that rushed out of our eyes came as we realized that we were not enough; so much more needed to be done. Yet, mixed in with our tears of sorrow and frustration were those of gratitude because we realized how much our lives were blessed by this community and its people.

"We were free to go back to our lives; Sonia and others were faced with hardships unsuitable to their ages. I think some of the tears we offered were about the unfairness of it all.

"Without power, without focus, we left the van, wiped our noses and eyes, and melted back into the crowd. Yet Melinda was determined to do something about it all.

"When Melinda returned home to Iowa, she refused to let the memory of Das Marinas die. She reached out to her community and shared her experiences in the Philippines, especially highlighting the situation of the children and why they needed financial support to stay in school. She showed courage, and she took risks to do that. In fact, M. Scott Peck said, "Love always requires courage and involves risk." Melinda was brave enough to risk rejection in her hometown due to the new ideas she was introducing and the need she was so trustingly asking her hometown to fill.

"Telling a neighbor that the amount needed to keep a child in school for a year was less than it cost to pay for a month's worth of coffee was thankfully convincing. Her message was simple and direct as she found ways to link her experience to the local lives of those in Iowa. When the good people of Iowa understood how they could help, they did.

"A scholarship fund was set up for the children of Das Marinas, and those who lived in Melinda's hometown were personally responsible for helping to start that fund. Melinda transformed those tears shed in Das Marinas into an action plan that resulted in Sonia and many other children having a chance at a brighter future.

"Melinda's actions served as a spiritual version of the International Bridge of Love. It is a bridge that went well beyond the physical limitations of cement and steel. This bridge crossed an ocean and improved the quality of life in two diverse communities. The main tool for creating this bridge was a heart filled with the creative power of love.

"Through the creative power of love, we also can build bridges. I wish you the best on your service projects from the bottom of my heart. May you know the blessings I have known in finding somewhere to help humanity just a little bit."

After the applause died down, the socializing began. Many expressions of mutual gratitude, love, and appreciation were exchanged. The students, one by one, hugged the Grandfather goodbye at this, their final class session with him. Slowly, regretfully, they began to wend their ways in small groups back to the school.

The Grandfather called out, "Chrissy? Did you want to speak to me for a moment?"

Chrissy smiled. "Actually, Grandfather, I think I have my answer."

He nodded sagely.

"Music is my gift," she explained. "It is a way I can serve. When I see the smiles on the faces of the people on the subway each day, I realize that it is a way to open people's hearts. It makes them blossom. It may not be as lucrative a career as engineering, but it is my form of service."

"Engineering is good too," mused the Grandfather. "It can build actual bridges. But I think you are right — the bridges you were designed to build are bridges to the human heart. I believe you are right that music is your path."

Mr. Bennet caught Chrissy and Juan's glances, and he gave them a distracted nod as he hurried to gather his things and catch up with the class. It was his responsibility to shepherd them safely back to school. Chrissy and Juan looked back at him solemnly, silently promising to return responsibly on their own, and he rushed off, enjoining Kyle to help him carry some things back to the school.

"You and I will talk, of course, Grandfather," Mr. Bennet said as he hurried off.

"Of course, my friend," said the Grandfather.

Chrissy and Juan stayed until the last streams of sunset coincided with the last notes of the songs of their instruments. Then they hugged the Grandfather, and Chrissy kissed him on the cheek.

"Come back when you will," said the Grandfather. "If you will. I know that life has a way of speeding up for young people, but any time you want to visit, you will be welcome."

"Even after I go away to college," said Chrissy, "I'll visit sometimes. And I'll always carry you in my heart."

"Me too," said Juan. "Wherever I go."

"Then I'll be contented," said the Grandfather. "To be a part of your journeys of the heart as you go about your lives of love and service."

About the Author

John W. Gehring, a teacher, trainer, lecturer, writer, and project director has worked on service, education, and sports programs in over 60 countries.

The author and his wife Yoshiko have five children, all of whom have worked on service projects and share a belief in the transformative power of love and service. At home and in his travels, his love for people has spanned countries, culture, and economic situations and has earned him the friendship of those he considers brother and sisters.

The book, *Tales of Love and Service: Stories from the Heart,* explores the everyday lives and challenges of parts of humanity that are often overlooked by those who may have grown too accustomed to the comforts of home. The author shares with readers not only the challenges that face those living in the grasp of Lady Poverty, but chronicles how the power of one person can inspire positive changes for many. He celebrates the triumph of the spirit in the characters in his stories.

John is moved by those who want to add meaning and value to their lives, and he hopes the unsung heroes you will meet in these stories will inspire as well as challenge you on your life's journey.

Made in the USA
Middletown, DE
29 July 2021